The Pocket Guide to Understanding ADHD

Practical tips for parents

DR CHRISTOPHER GREEN
and DR KIT CHEE

DOUBLEDAY
SYDNEY • AUCKLAND • TORONTO • NEW YORK • LONDON

THE POCKET GUIDE TO UNDERSTANDING ADHD
A DOUBLEDAY BOOK

First published in Australia and New Zealand in 2004
by Doubleday

Text copyright © Dr Christopher Green, 2004
Illustrations copyright © Roger Roberts, 1994 and 2004

National Library of Australia
Cataloguing-in-Publication Entry

    Green, Christopher, 1943 Feb. 23- .
    The pocket guide to understanding ADHD : practical tips for
    parents.

    ISBN 1 86471 089 6.

    1. Attention-deficit hyperactivity disorder – Popular works.
    2. Attention-deficit-disordered children. 3. Child
    rearing. I. Title. II. Title : The pocket guide to
    understanding Attention Deficit Hyperactivity Disorder.

    618.928589

Transworld Publishers,
a division of Random House Australia Pty Ltd
20 Alfred Street, Milsons Point, NSW 2061
http://www.randomhouse.com.au

Random House New Zealand Limited
18 Poland Road, Glenfield, Auckland

Transworld Publishers,
a division of The Random House Group Ltd
61-63 Uxbridge Road, Ealing, London W5 5SA

Random House Inc
1745 Broadway, New York, New York 10036

Edited by Vanessa Hill
Cover design by Darian Causby/Highway 51 Design Works
Cover illustration by Roger Roberts
Text designed and typeset in 10.3/14 Stone Serif by Midland Typesetters, Maryborough, Victoria
Printed and bound by Griffin Press

Contents

About the Authors

Dr Christopher Green MB, BCh, BAO, FRACP, MRCP(UK), FRCP(I), DCH, OAM

Christopher Green is a paediatrician and honorary consultant to the Children's Hospital, Westmead, in Sydney. Over the past 15 years, Dr Green has been prominent in introducing modern attitudes towards treatment of ADHD to Australia, New Zealand and the UK.

Dr Kit Y Chee MB, BS, Phd, FRACP

Kit Chee is a specialist paediatrician at the Sydney Learning Clinic and honorary consultant at the Children's Hospital, Westmead. She has a doctorate in language, learning and handwriting disorders in children with ADHD.

Introduction

Attention Deficit Hyperactivity Disorder (ADHD) is a slight but demonstrable difference in brain function. It causes a clever child to underachieve academically and behave poorly, despite the highest standard of parenting.

The Pocket Guide to Understanding ADHD puts all the facts at parents' fingertips. We discuss the main behaviours associated with ADHD: a child who doesn't know when to put the brakes on behaviour, who puts in so much effort and gets so little reward, who is often known by all yet liked by none and, perhaps most importantly, makes competent parents appear inadequate.

We have come a long way in understanding this hard-to-define condition. The danger for today's parents and professionals is to become lost in the uncertainties, rather than focusing on what we know to be true and using this information to help our children.

If managing ADHD was easy, there would be no need for this book. The aim of *The Pocket Guide to Understanding ADHD* is to make a complex subject easier to digest. If you would like more detailed information (including the latest research) after reading this book, move on to *Understanding ADHD*.

ONE

ADHD – The Facts

CLASS OF 2004

With so much current interest in ADHD you might think that we are in the midst of an epidemic. But ADHD is occurring no more frequently than in the past – we have just become more skilful at recognising a very real condition that was previously missed or misdiagnosed.

ADHD is a 'mixed bag' of behaviours: attention, hyperactivity, learning, the list goes on. So this chapter looks straight to the facts about ADHD.

The facts about ADHD

- ADHD is a real condition that to some extent affects approximately 2 to 5 per cent of all children.

- ADHD is a biological, brain-based condition which is caused by a minor difference of fine tuning in the normal brain (a slight brain dysfunction).

- The dysfunction of ADHD is thought to be due to an imbalance in the brain's neurotransmitter chemicals, noradrenaline and dopamine. This imbalance is mostly found in those parts of the brain responsible for self-monitoring and putting on the brakes.

- ADHD presents in two ways: in impulsive, poorly self-monitored behaviour (referred to as hyperactive–

impulsive behaviour), and in problems of attention, short-term memory, disorganisation and learning (attention deficit–learning problems). A child may have just one of these forms, but most ADHD children have a mixture of both.

An ADHD child is significantly out of step with others of the same developmental level and standard of parenting.

- These behaviours and learning problems are not exclusive to ADHD. They occur in all of us, but to a much lesser extent.

- ADHD is a strongly hereditary condition. Most ADHD children have a close relative (usually male) affected to some degree by the same problem. Developmental Reading Disorder (dyslexia) which is often associated with ADHD is also a strongly hereditary condition.

- ADHD is mostly a 'boy' problem. Boys are six times more likely to be referred for help than girls. However, it's possible that the true ratio in the community is more like 3:1, as many girls remain undiagnosed – by nature girls tend to be less disruptive and suffer more silently than the male of the species. They may not be referred to a clinic for bad behaviour, but they may still be failing at school.

■ ADHD is a long-term condition which affects learning and behaviour right through the school years. About 60–70 per cent of these children will carry some of their ADHD with them into adulthood.

■ Some preschoolers are incorrectly labelled as 'hyperactive'. In fact they have no problem other than the normal 'busyness' and lack of commonsense one finds at this young age. (See *Toddler Taming* for more about this age group.)

■ Most parents first suspect their ADHD child is out of step between the age of two-and-a-half and three years. However, the more laid-back, less demanding life of preschool means that most of these children manage well until the first or second year of school.

■ Teachers of ADHD children tell us that at school: 'This child is distractable, disruptive and needs one-to-one supervision to achieve'. Teachers are confused when a clever child behaves poorly and underfunctions for intellect.

Diet is no longer seen as an important part of ADHD.

- Playground problems are common as the child misreads social cues, 'comes on too strong', and overreacts to teasing. This has immense implications for self-esteem.

  Sometimes teachers describe an ADHD child as 'known by all but liked by none'.

- ADHD children do not plan to behave badly, it just seems to happen and after the event they feel true remorse.

- Approximately half of the children who present with ADHD are also troubled by specific learning disabilities (SLD), for example dyslexia, Language Disorder or a weakness with mathematics. These are not caused by the ADHD but are associated or 'comorbid' conditions. The treatment of ADHD does not treat the SLD, but it makes the child more receptive to remedial teaching.

- At school the two parts of ADHD (hyperactive–impulsive behaviour and attention deficit–learning problems) show in different ways. The hyperactive–impulsive, poor self-monitoring behaviours result in the child rushing through work, settling slowly after a break, tapping and fidgeting, calling out in class and failing to check work before it is handed in. The attention deficit problems affect organisation, getting started with work, listening skills, sustained work output, distractability and short-term memory.

■ Poor impulse control leaves the ADHD child both physically and verbally accident-prone. They frequently trip, fall, act stupid and put their 'feet in their mouth'. ADHD children nag and demand from dawn to dusk – this incessant pressure generates great tension.

■ Most ADHD children have the social and emotional maturity of a child two-thirds their age. Lack of emotional understanding, independence and commonsense are frequent complaints.

■ Treatment of ADHD involves behavioural advice, support at school and the use of stimulant medication.

■ ADHD children act before they think and are less satisfied with rewards. This makes the behavioural techniques that work so well on our other children much less effective when used on those with ADHD.

In ADHD it is the difficult child that makes good, competent parents appear inadequate.

■ Stimulant medication is effective in the treatment

of ADHD. Their benefits in treating ADHD have been well known for more than 50 years. More recently a major US multi-centre study completed in 1999 looked at the relative benefits of

Stimulants help a child to focus, listen and be reached. You have to reach before you can teach.

various combinations of medical, educational and psychological treatments for ADHD. The results suggest that without first priming with medication, most of the other techniques are relatively ineffective.

- Stimulant medication is often misrepresented but it is without doubt the single most effective form of therapy available for ADHD.

- The stimulants methylphenidate (Ritalin) and dexamphetamine have been used for more than 40 years. At the last count there have been more than 170 controlled trials which show their benefits and safety.

- Stimulants are not addictive. Medication brings the unfocused child into full-focus reality. You don't get addicted to reality.

- Natural remedies are often promoted as safer than stimulants and equally effective in the ADHD child. These have not been subjected to the same scientific trials and safety checks that would be required for a medication. Just because a product comes from a plant does not mean it is safe: opium, digitalis, magic mushrooms and tobacco are all natural substances.

■ If there is ever any doubt about benefits or any worrying side-effect, the parents must stop the preparation at once and talk to those who prescribed it.

■ With any medical treatment the benefits must be carefully balanced against all potential risks. Critics of medication quote the obscure, small print side-effects but do not mention the major risk of failing to treat. Every year impulsive, unthinking ADHD children are injured or killed needlessly in accidents. Countless families of untreated children fall out of love with the difficult child and these wrecked relationships may never heal.

Medication is only prescribed after a full explanation and the informed consent of the parents. Parents are in charge, not doctors.

■ The ADHD child is not deliberately difficult, they just act before they think. Successful parents make allowances but still ensure that children with ADHD know they are responsible for their own actions. ADHD is an explanation, it is not an excuse.

TWO

ADHD – An Old Condition Rediscovered

ADHD has been heavily promoted recently in the popular press but it is not a new condition. ADHD was first described in 1902. Some of the most influential people of all time had one thing in common: they channelled their ADHD activity, drive and single-mindedness to achieve greatness.

During the past 100 years, the definition of ADHD began as a cluster of behaviours that were of biological (inborn) origin and had a poor prognosis. Later, experts believed that ADHD might be caused by brain damage. Next all the focus was on hyperactivity. Then diet seemed all-important in a condition that was believed to resolve itself before high school age. The current definition describes a cluster of inbuilt behaviours of which inattention is paramount and impulsivity and overactivity are usual. The problems are long term and symptoms often continue into adulthood. Medication is now accepted as an important part of therapy.

Famous ADHD sufferers include Winston Churchill and Albert Einstein.

We have come a long way, but ADHD remains a highly variable, complex and imprecisely defined condition. The danger for today's parents and professionals is to become lost in the uncertainties, rather than focusing on what we know to be true and using this information to help our children.

100 years of ADHD

1902:	Clear description of ADHD behaviours.
1930s:	Brain damage believed to cause ADHD behaviours.
1937:	Stimulant medication first used.
1950s–60s:	Now believed to be a brain dysfunction ('Minimal Brain Dysfunction').
	Psychoanalytical child psychiatrists see ADHD as a parent and environment problem (for some, this attitude continued until the 1990s).
1957:	Methylphenidate (Ritalin) introduced.
1960–70:	The 'Hyperactive Child Syndrome' theory becomes popular. Ritalin widely used and many research papers on stimulants are published.
1970–75:	Inaccurate media claims raise concerns with medication.
	Feingold Diet becomes popular.
1975–80:	Medication regains considerable popularity.
1980:	The American Psychiatric Association (APA) uses term 'Attention Deficit Disorder'.

1987: The APA uses term 'Attention Deficit Hyperactivity Disorder'. Anti-medication campaign misleads many parents and professionals.

1990: Positron Emission Tomography (PET scan) shows significant difference in function between the ADHD brain and the non-ADHD brain.

1994: The APA redefines the term 'Attention Deficit Hyperactivity Disorder'.

1997: ADHD seen as an interplay of four factors: attention and learning; impulsive, poorly controlled behaviours; the presence or absence of comorbid conditions; nurture or hostility in the child's environment.

2004: Converging evidence from molecular genetics, neurotransmitter research, brain scans, EEG, and studies across cultures authenticate the validity of ADHD.

THREE

ADHD – The Cause

Researchers still disagree on the exact cause of ADHD, but two things are certain: firstly, that it is a hereditary condition and secondly, that the problems of ADHD result from a subtle difference in the fine tuning of the brain. It is also believed that parenting may contribute to some extent. And, finally, it is possible that ADHD is just part of the normal spectrum of temperaments.

ADHD is definitely NOT caused by diet or by poor parenting.

Most of the current debate centres around the exact nature of this brain difference. Some doctors see ADHD as a part of the normal range of temperament, but the majority believe that it is a syndrome which is separate from temperament. Most researchers now believe that it is due to the underfunctioning of those areas of the brain that put the brakes on unwise behaviour: the frontal lobes and their close connections the basal ganglia and cerebellar circuits. There also seems to exist an unusual imbalance in the message-transmitting chemicals of the brain, the neurotransmitters.

Heredity – genes and ADHD

When we look carefully at families, we notice that most children with ADHD have a close relative with a similar problem. Often we see a father who found his early school years difficult or who underfunctioned academically for his abilities. Some of these adults have done well in life but are still restless, inattentive and fitted with a dangerously short fuse.

Why one child in a family inherits ADHD and another does not, depends on which genes they inherited from their parents.

There is good research evidence to prove this genetic influence. Identical twins share the same genetic material. If one twin suffers ADHD, research shows there is an almost 90 per cent chance the other will also have this problem.

Non-identical twins have the same risk of ADHD as the brother or sister of any ADHD child. The risk between siblings is somewhere between 30 and 40 per cent. These are high figures when compared with the normal rate of ADHD of between 2 and 5 per cent in the general population. An ADHD child of a parent with both ADHD and dyslexia often inherits both problems.

The brain difference

In this noisy world, most of the unimportant messages that enter into the brain are screened out at a low level without ever coming to the attention of 'middle management'. Important information is taken in and looked at by the specialist parts of the brain, which interact together to give a properly co-ordinated response. Finally, the chief executive (frontal lobe) takes an overview of the middle management decisions, approving or disapproving on the grounds of appropriateness, priorities, future implications and their effect on others.

In the ADHD child's brain, however, information seems to rush in without much filtering, which leaves the television screen of the mind in a bit of a buzz. The information is integrated, but action is often taken before the chief executive has approved the decision.

Parenting and ADHD

Children with ADHD often behave badly and cause stress for their parents. The normal methods of discipline work less well for these children, and after some years of failure most parents back off and aim for the more peaceful path. Then some shortsighted experts, noting this lack of textbook disciple, attribute the child's behaviour to poor parental management.

It is important for every professional to realise that

a child's behaviour affects the style of disciplining, just as the parent's discipline affects the style of behaviour.

Genuine parenting problems

Where major family chaos exists, this will affect any child, whether they have ADHD or not. Statistics show that ADHD children have a greater chance of coming from a dysfunctional home setting. On face value it would be easy to see this family turmoil as the sole cause of the difficult behaviour, but things are not always what they seem.

We know that major troubles in the home are much more likely if a parent has an intolerant, impulsive, socially inept style of temperament. These problems of personality make an adult hard to live with, but they may also be symptoms of residual ADHD.

This is where the confusion really starts. If a parent has ADHD, the child is at risk of inheriting the same condition. If this genetically more difficult child is then brought up in a home which is inconsistent, volatile and full of stress, the behaviour will be blown through the roof.

Which came first – the chicken or the egg? Genes and environment may both be responsible.

ADHD – normal, not pathological

Research from the late 1950s shows that each child is born with an individual temperamental style. Could it be that ADHD is just part of the wide spectrum of normal temperament? ADHD behaviours may even have been of benefit in the past.

Until recent times, reading, writing and sitting in a classroom would have been irrelevant for the average child and ADHD would probably not have been noticed. Going even further back, ADHD may have been an advantage in caveman times, when survival was all-important. While cooking a rabbit over a fire our ADHD ancestors would be quickly distracted by every breaking twig and rustle in the bushes. If danger appeared they would respond by reflex. On the other hand, our deep-thinking, attentive ancestors might focus so much on the rabbit, that they would be wiped out before they knew of the danger. Possibly these active, impulsive people were the super-humans of their day, while those who are now well-behaved school achievers would have been quite disabled.

Active, impulsive behaviours may have been an asset for our ancestors.

We know that Winston Churchill underfunctioned at school, but the immense energy and bloody-mindedness of his ADHD changed the course of history. ADHD is not due to a damaged brain, but it is probably an edge of the wide spectrum of normal. In the past it may have been an attribute, but today the demands of school and society have turned it into a problem.

ADHD in brief

1. A hereditary condition

- When a parent and child both have ADHD it is because of shared genes.

- Usually a parent or close relative has ADHD.

- If a parent has ADHD and SLD, the child will often inherit both.

- In studies of identical twins, if one has ADHD, there is a 90 per cent chance the other will also.

- Siblings carry a 30–40 per cent risk of inheriting ADHD.

2. A problem of fine tuning of the brain

- Impulsive ADHD children show frontal lobe dysfunction: they can't 'put the brakes' on behaviour.

■ Children who are purely inattentive (without impulsive, active behaviour) show the same frontal lobe problems but also have a slow processing speed: 'slow moving cogs'.

3. Parenting and ADHD

■ Poor parenting does not *cause* ADHD, but can make the behaviour worse.

■ Difficult children make their parents' discipline appear inadequate.

■ Major family dysfunction can occur with ADHD: part of the problem may be in the genes and part in the environment.

4. Maybe we're wrong

■ It could just be a part of temperament.

■ Pressure of nowadays versus thousands of years ago.

FOUR

The Behaviours that Bother Parents

The aim of this chapter is to paint a technicolour picture of how ADHD children seem to their parents and teachers. Once you recognise the shades that make up this disorder, move to Chapter 5 to see how these fit in with the modern view of ADHD.

The behaviours that cause concern are: inattentiveness, impulsiveness, overactivity, insatiability, social clumsiness, poor co-ordination, disorganisation, variability poor self-esteem and specific learning disabilities (SLD).

Inattentiveness

The inattentive child quickly loses the focus of their attention. They become bored, get distracted and may flit from task to task without achieving anything. Schoolwork takes a long time to complete or never gets finished. Teachers are mystified; the child does so much when they are stood over and so little when they are left alone.

This deficit varies from day to day: some days these children are in tune, and the next they are 'off the planet'. This behaviour also changes from one situation to another; some of the most inattentive children we manage can leave their peers for dead as they focus on a video game.

This variability means inattention may often be missed by inexperienced assessors. Some ADHD children appear to concentrate well in the novel, interesting environment of the specialist's office. Some equally inattentive children work well with the psychologist in one-to-one testing but fall apart when they return to a busy class of 30.

Inattention to verbal instructions and a poor short-term memory are particular problems. Parents send the child off to get two things, they reappear a minute later and say, 'What was the second one?'

There is an interesting subgroup of inattentive children (ADHD – inattentive only type) who are heavily distracted by their own thoughts. These children appear to drift off the air as their teacher starts to talk. Their minds are a million miles away and as they sit placidly in class they cause no one any bother, but they don't seem to learn. They become 'the quiet unachievers'.

Adults with residual ADHD often tell of their difficulty concentrating during a lecture. Others cope with their poor

Einstein was probably a quiet unachiever: an intelligent school failure more interested in cracking the theory of relativity than in listening to his teacher.

short-term memory by doing things immediately or writing reminder notes. Most of these inattentive adults and children have difficulty with mental arithmetic or remembering a sequence of numbers.

It's hard to communicate with an inattentive child, and stimulant medication may help this problem. One of our patients once said, 'At school, when I don't take my pill, lots of people are talking. When I do, I only hear the teacher.'

What the parents say

'What I tell him goes in one ear and out the other. Can we get his hearing tested?'

'With homework I get nowhere unless I stand over him.'

'He's impossible in the morning. He goes to his room to get ready for school, half an hour later he has one sock on and is looking out the window.'

'He can remember details of what happened last year but forgets what I said two minutes ago.'

Inattention is not always ADHD

When any of us find our work too difficult, we quickly lose concentration. This is called secondary inattention and is found in children who have problems of language, reading, writing or mathematics. The child switches off when their mind is overloaded, but full attention returns once the stress stops.

Children who are intellectually disabled often appear inattentive, but their attention span is appropriate for their younger developmental age. Other children drift off when their mind is preoccupied by some stress, but this comes and goes with emotional events and is not associated with the other cluster of ADHD behaviours. There are, of course, occasions when emotional stress, specific learning problems and intellectual disability can coexist with ADHD.

Impulsiveness

ADHD children do not set out to get into trouble, they just shoot straight from the hip with no thought of the repercussions. These children are quite aware of what is right and wrong, but it doesn't register until a millisecond after they have reacted and by then it is too late.

Poor impulse control is the behaviour that gets these children into the most trouble. Parents can't understand how someone so intelligent can behave so stupidly. No amount of reasoning helps the situation; the children are genuinely upset at what they've done but they will be just as unthinking the next time.

When the average child is shoved at assembly, they carefully check if the teacher is looking before they kick someone in retaliation. The ADHD child responds by reflex, gets caught and is called aggressive.

Many ADHD children are 'accident-prone'; they run across roads and ride their bicycles without looking ahead.

Impulsive children interrupt and talk over the top of others. They are also easily frustrated and extremely impatient. Most have a short fuse and explode easily.

In school, incorrect answers are blurted out before the question has been completed. Instructions are only half heard before a response is made. Work is rushed through with lots of careless mistakes.

In the playground, these children are easily led and often over the top. Some have such poor playground behaviour that they spend most lunchtimes sitting outside the principal's office. These children are not aggressive, but their behaviour quickly escalates out of control and they don't think too deeply of the consequences of their actions. A number of older children find themselves suspended from school after a poorly managed blow-up.

These sparky, 'short fuse' children are difficult to discipline as their reactions are so reflex-bound. They learn slowly from experience and along the way cause great pain to their parents, teachers and themselves.

What the parents say

'He doesn't seem to learn from experience.'

'She's eight but she still interrupts us like a toddler.'

'At school other children seek him out to taunt. They know he will always react.'

'He's got such a short fuse – it's like juggling gelignite.'

'We worry that one of these days he's going to get a driving licence!'

Overactivity

Historically, it is hyperactive behaviour which has been the main feature of ADHD. It is our opinion that overactivity in isolation is only a minor problem, but when overactivity and impulsivity come together, this busy, short-fused combination becomes absolute dynamite.

A few of these restless young people were unusually active even before they were born. A significant number were colicky and demanding in infancy. A surprising proportion were quite average or even exceptionally good as babies – presumably they were saving themselves! For most parents the change came when they started to walk; then they took the house apart and got into everything.

Most are busy at preschool, finding it hard to settle at storytime. Once school starts, hyperactivity is generally more subtle in its presentation. There is an overall increase in body movement, which gets worse as the day wears on. These children are restless, fidget and have difficulty remaining seated. Those who appear to be sitting still are jiggling their legs, tapping their fingers or fiddling with anything they can touch. This restless squirming activity is described as 'rump hyperactivity'. These school children may not move from their seat, but their rump and fingers are certainly pretty active.

When busy children hit the playground they are like an animal released from captivity. When they return to the structure of the classroom, many find it hard to settle. At home they pace around, touch things, open and close the refrigerator door. Hyperactivity tends to ease in the early school years and is much less by the time these young people reach teen age. A few remain just as fast and furious in their adult years.

What the parents say

'He was hyperactive even before he was born.'
   'This toddler is constantly on the move.'
   'When visiting he has to touch everything.'
   'He is a teenager, but on a wet day he still paces around like a caged animal.'
   'His grandmother says I was just the same as a child.'

Insatiability

These children intrude, demand, interrogate and don't know when to back off. This insatiability is probably the most nerve-numbing behaviour for parents. Once an idea gets into their mind, these children go on and on, long past the point when any other child would have let it drop.

It is a minute before dinner: 'Can I have a slice of bread?' 'No, your dinner is just about ready.' 'Can I have a biscuit?' 'No!' 'Can I have a banana?' Soon their parent is ready for a straitjacket.

They quibble, nag and rabbit on until the calmest parent is close to having a stroke. Insatiability is the behaviour that causes the greatest stress – at the end of a family weekend the parents feel as if they have had a 48-hour work-out with the KGB.

When stimulant medication is effective most parents spontaneously say that home life has become calmer. Easing the escalation and interrogation is what they mean.

What the parents say

'Why can't she put a lid on it?'

'Nothing I do pleases him; whatever he gets, he wants more.'

'We don't tell him when we are going on a trip. If we did he would ask, "Are we going on Wednesday? How will we get there? Are we really going on Wednesday? Are we going by car? Is it Wednesday we're going?".'

'I try to stay calm, but as he goes on and on, my chest feels tight, my neck tenses and I wonder if I'm about to have a coronary.'

Social clumsiness

Though ADHD children are sensitive and caring, many are socially out of tune. They want to be popular with their mates but don't seem to know how to make this happen. They misread the accepted social cues, saying or doing something quite inappropriate. In the group they come on too strong, which makes their friends pull away and wonder 'What sort of a weirdo is this?'.

In the playground they want to be part of the main game, but rather than let things take their natural course, they barge in, poke, taunt and annoy. The more they try to be friendly, the more they become isolated.

These children function best in the small group setting or with one good friend. Even here they can have problems, being bossy and always wanting to be top dog. Friends who come around to play soon leave in a huff.

Social problems hit a peak in primary school and start to ease in high school. In adolescence, however, any

What the parents say

'Other children don't seem to understand him.'

'He's so hurt by being shunned by his schoolmates, though he brings it on himself.'

'He says he has no friends.'

'Before medication he was the only member of the class who was never asked to a birthday party. This year he's been to seven!'

'At times he's quite paranoid. The most innocent things others do are interpreted as deliberate attempts to get at him.'

remaining insecurities make the normal social uncertainties of this age even greater. When adults bring the remains of their ADHD to their grown-up years it is often this social clumsiness that causes particular pain.

Poor co-ordination

Co-ordination problems show in fine motor tasks (colouring, manipulating, handwriting, tying shoelaces) and gross motor tasks (running, climbing, catching a ball, riding a bike).

Most ADHD children have difficulty with fine motor tasks, particularly handwriting. The further they get down the page, the greater the untidiness and the more they cross out. Parents and teachers often despair over the quality of this handwork, becoming so obsessed with the writing they fail to spot the talent in the content.

A few ADHD children are genuinely clumsy but a larger number appear clumsy due to their poor impulse control. These children charge around like a bull in a china shop, bumping, tripping and spilling as they go. Their knees and elbows are scarred, their lower legs covered with bruises.

Many ADHD children have a less obvious co-ordination

What the parents say

'He's so clumsy, he's last to be picked for any game.'

'I know you tell me her co-ordination is normal but the way she moves is different from other children.'

'Soccer does not suit: he forgets what he is doing and goes walkabout.'

'If there was one small brick in a big playground, she would trip over it.'

problem – they have difficulty co-ordinating a sequence of movements or doing two things at the one time. At the swimming pool they move their arms and kick their legs, but they don't seem able to breathe in rhythm. At the dance class they love the music but when it comes to formal steps they are lost. Shoelaces are abandoned in favour of Velcro.

When children have difficulty throwing and catching a ball, they feel unwelcome in the normal school-break play activities. However, with a good occupational therapist they can improve their performance in the playground. On the positive side, many ADHD children are superb at sports, and this attribute gives an immense uplift to their self-esteem.

Some adults with ADHD are exceptional athletes. One

of Australia's rugby greats was recently in trouble for impulsive outbursts on the field. A friend who gave a character reference said, 'He is a wonderful guy, but like a large international airport with a very small control tower'.

Disorganisation

Many ADHD children are highly disorganised. You can see this in their dress: clothes are back to front, inside out and messy, while shoelaces are only half tied. Dirty hands wipe through the hair and over the clothes, and some have 'fiddly fingers', which seem to act without instruction from the brain.

What the parents say

'If I ask him to tuck in his shirt, the shirt goes in. As he removes his hand, twice as much comes out.'

'Everything he touches is sticky.'

'When doing homework she lines up her books, takes out a pencil, sharpens it, puts it away, takes out another and just can't get started.'

'He's so disorganised, he's the sort of child who could eat a Mars Bar and brush his teeth at the same time!'

Messages sent from school never get home. The school bag is left on the bus. Swimming costumes are found later at the pool. Books are not brought home for homework. Many children are blind to the trail of mess that surrounds them.

By the early high school years, ADHD children are generally tidier, but disorganisation is still an impediment. When doing projects, they fiddle, procrastinate and find it hard to get things started. During exams, they spend half their time on one question and don't finish the other questions. Many ADHD adults acknowledge this vulnerability and protect themselves by living life to a strict, almost obsessive, routine.

When an ADHD child is disorganised from birth, their messiness will improve with age, and it is important that parents do not get too worked up along the way. When an obsessively tidy mother produces a completely disorganised child there is the potential for major conflict. Fighting is pointless, as no amount of nagging will change this child in the short term.

Variability

All children and adults have good and bad days, but people with ADHD experience extreme variation in

What the parents say

'Some days she is so easy to be with. Others she just doesn't know what to be up to.'

'Homework is usually a hassle, then some days he finishes it in 10 minutes.'

'On bad days his teacher sends him to help in the library. She realises he is learning nothing in the classroom.'

'His emotions are all over the place. One minute he's intensely irritating, the next he's devastated at a minor reprimand.'

performance and mood. These dramatic differences confuse parents, who have often asked if their child might have a double personality or even be schizophrenic!

Parents try to account for the bad days by blaming stress, lack of sleep or some dietary difference. Even when these factors are carefully controlled, the behavioural fluctuations will remain. Their cause is not known, but they are certainly not intentional.

Teachers are particularly aware of this variation. On the occasional good day they are amazed at how so much work can be achieved. On bad days they say that the child might as well have stayed at home. Teachers have to accept that these fluctuations will occur and reward the occasional good day. The bad days have to be accepted as part of ADHD and not as a sign of laziness.

Poor self-esteem

It is a paradox, but most ADHD children are exceptionally sensitive. For this reason it is important to look below all their hustle and hype to see the soft, sensitive centre.

Self-esteem is almost always low in ADHD children – it's no surprise, as they experience so much failure. They put so much effort in to their schoolwork, yet achieve so little. They want to be popular, but they are treated like an annoying outcast. Some achieve well at games, while others are banished to the sideline, as being too 'unco' (unco-ordinated) to play with their mates.

This combination of sensitivity, vulnerability and inadequate esteem in those with ADHD must be taken seriously. By the age of 20 all their classroom problems will have settled, but any ongoing weakness in socialisation and self-esteem will have implications for the rest of their lives.

What the parents say

'He says he's dumb.'

'She tells me she has no friends.'

'He says he's ugly.'

'She now gives up without even trying.'

'He finds it easier to hang out with younger children or others with problems.'

Specific learning disabilities (SLD)

Over half of all children with ADHD will have a significant weakness in some academic area. This may be in reading, writing, spelling, language, mathematics or a combination of all of these skills. These problems of learning and language are so frequently associated with ADHD that it is important to consider them in every child. It is tough at school when you can't concentrate, organise your work and stick at a task. It is even tougher when there are also unrecognised problems of learning and language.

When is it normal? When is it ADHD?

As you have read the list of behaviours covered in this chapter, we can hear you say, 'But these are

What the parents say

'He has such difficulty with spelling.'

'She's a very slow reader.'

'He just doesn't get maths.'

'His words are all jumbled and make no sense most of the time.'

present in lots of normal children and adults'. That's true: *there is no clear cut-off point between the normal child with an active temperament and the one with a mild ADHD.*

The diagnosis will be made by looking at which behaviours predominate, their magnitude and how well they are being handled. No one is going to set up a behavioural program or give medication unnecessarily. We treat only those whose behaviour and learning are causing problems to themselves and those who care for them. The difference between the bothersome behaviour of ADHD and that of a normal, busy temperament is the trouble it creates.

Remember: 'A problem is only a problem when it causes a problem'.

The next chapter shows how the problems of attention, behaviour, learning disability, defiance and factors in the child's environment all fit together.

FIVE

ADHD – A Four-Part Problem

When a group of parents discuss their ADHD children, any eavesdropper would realise that no two are identical. Some of these children are amazingly active, interrogative and impulsive. Some are inattentive and dreamy, while the behaviour of others is hostile and oppositional. Many are dyslexic, some have language problems

ADHD is a bit of a mixed bag.

and most are underfunctioning at school. Occasionally an older child is involved in criminal activities.

What those parents are seeing is a blend of four parts, only two of which correctly fit the ADHD diagnosis. These are hyperactive–impulsive behaviours and attention deficit–learning problems.

In our practice, we see two other parts to ADHD. These are not *caused* by ADHD, but are likely to present *with* ADHD. The third part of ADHD is a group of associated problems (called comorbid conditions), for example dyslexia, Oppositional Defiant Disorder (ODD) and Conduct Disorder (CD). These are not caused by ADHD but occur in more than half of these children.

And just when you thought you understood what was going on, the fourth part of ADHD, the standard of support in the child's environment, adds further problems. Again, this is not caused by ADHD but can confuse the problem for both parent and child.

ADHD – the four parts

The first two parts – true ADHD (*this chapter*)

- Part 1: hyperactive–impulsive behaviours (rushing through work, trouble settling, forgets).

- Part 2: attention deficit–learning problems (poor organisation, slow starting, distracted, problems of short-term memory).

Note: Most ADHD children have a mix of both parts to varying degrees, though some may have one part in isolation (eg inattentive only).

The third part – comorbid conditions (see *Chapter 6*)

- Over half those with ADHD have an associated (comorbid) condition.

- Those conditions include specific learning disabilities, Oppositional Defiant Disorder Conduct Disorder, Tic Disorder, poor co-ordination, depression, anxiety, Obsessive Compulsive Disorder and Bipolar Disorder.

The fourth part – the child's support environment (see *Chapter 7*)

- Supportive parenting versus hostile, critical parenting.

- Supportive schooling versus unaccepting education.

- An extended stable family versus isolation and rejection.

In this chapter, we are talking about the first two parts of ADHD only.

True ADHD

Thirty-five years ago ADHD, or Hyperactivity as it was then known, was all about restless, busy behaviours – but now we realise that activity by itself is not the problem.

Nowadays ADHD is accepted as these two parts, the hyperactive–impulsive (HI) behaviours and attention deficit–learning problems. Most ADHD children show some degree of attention deficit–learning problems as well as HI behaviours. A significant (and probably under-estimated) number have only the deficit in attention, short-term memory and learning. A minority have only the HI behaviours.

Hyperactive–impulsive behaviours

A child with HI behaviours intrudes into every aspect of our lives. They are fidgety, restless, impulsive and impatient. Parents are amazed that **'He doesn't put the brakes on behaviour.'** their apparently intelligent child can do such stupid things: 'I constantly worry what he is up to.' 'He doesn't seem to learn from his mistakes.' 'He doesn't seem to know when to back off.' 'He doesn't see how he's annoying other people.' 'He is funny the first time but just keeps going until everyone is sick of him.'

These parents are talking about a problem of inadequate self-control. The HI behaviours that most trouble parents were described in Chapter 4.

Attention deficit–learning problems

We all suffer the occasional lapse in attention and learning, but in ADHD this causes clever children to underfunction in school and life. Those who see attention deficit as just an inability to concentrate have a very simplistic view of the situation.

Underfocus/overfocus

The inattentive part of ADHD is not simply a matter of flitting and lack of focus. The problems of attention are influenced by specific situations. The child may be inattentive at school, but give them a computer game or a goal to mind and they never miss a point. Some with ADHD get stuck on one idea, can't take a step back and see the big picture. With them ADHD is not just 'under-attention', it is also 'overattention'. They can't let go of an idea and will pursue it past all reason.

The stimulant drugs improve the ability to focus, disengage and refocus.

Getting started and keeping going

The ADHD mind is bursting with bright ideas – the problem is putting them into action. Things generally go well in the early years of education, but this changes when self-motivation, time management and completing projects become important. The inattentive procrastinates, fiddles, time-wastes and makes any excuse to avoid starting. Their work output is uneven, with great bursts of enthusiasm followed by times of little action.

Many ADHD teenagers and adults are at their most productive with the adrenalin rush of a last-minute deadline.

A restless, circling brain

The inattentive becomes bored unless work is new, varied and closely supervised. There is great difficulty sustaining effort when performing routine, monotonous tasks. Some adults and children experience

Those with ADHD don't need others to distract them, they distract themselves!

immense drowsiness as their interest fades. Pages of print pass their eyes but nothing seems to register.

The inattentive finds it hard to regroup after interruptions. It is not only outside events that steal their concentration – the restless, constantly circling brain of ADHD is always scanning to find new areas of focus.

This fast-moving, ever-circling brain gives the person with ADHD an immense ability to create. Unfortunately the lack of executive control can prevent this creativity being translated into royalties.

Drifting and 'spacing'

Some children with the 'inattentive only' form of ADHD are dreamy, drifty 'space men'. Their brains seem to move slowly, but these children are often unnoticed at school as they behave well and fail in silence. This dreamy form of ADHD is made much worse by its strong association with specific learning disabilities, particularly dyslexia.

Teachers become exasperated as they try to get through to these quiet non-achievers.

This form of ADHD is currently creating great interest. It's probably much more common than we realise and may be a frequent cause of school failure in that gentle ADHD population – girls.

Retaining and remembering

One of the greatest frustrations for anyone with attention deficit is its effect on short-term memory. You remember the finest detail of the trip you took two years ago, but nothing of the instruction just given. Parents can't understand how a clever child can be so unaware of what has just been said and so forgetful.

We have seen wives arrange a hearing test, as they believe their ADHD husbands must be deaf!

With reading, the child has forgotten what was at the top of the paragraph by the time they reach the bottom. Memorising times tables, doing homework and learning lists are all a hassle. As they close their books in the evening the information is in their head, but it evaporates before the test the next day.

No amount of aggravation by teachers, parents or loved ones will change the 'easy come – easy go' memory of ADHD. This is frustrating not only for parents and teachers but also for the ADHD student.

Now that we have a grip on the different components that make up true ADHD, let's introduce two additional factors to the equation: the associated conditions, or comorbidities (Chapter 6), and the support environment (Chapter 7).

Children with ADHD can put in so much effort and get so little reward.

SIX

Associated Conditions

We have seen that the condition we call ADHD is made up of various blends and severities of attention deficit–learning problems and hyperactive–impulsive behaviours.

The presence of ADHD greatly increases the coexistence of associated or comorbid conditions. These include specific learning disabilities (SLD), Oppositional Defiant Disorder (ODD), Conduct Disorder (CD), depression, tics, Tourette syndrome and co-ordination problems. The ADHD does not *cause* the oppositional behaviour, dyslexia or the tics, they are just more likely to coexist.

As these associated problems occur in more than half those with ADHD, this means that much of what is called ADHD is in fact a comorbid condition. It is important to recognise these common associations, as different treatments are needed for each problem.

Comorbidity and professional blindness

Over the years the understanding of ADHD has been obstructed by professionals who have looked at ADHD with tunnel vision. They believed that if a child had ODD this ruled out the diagnosis of ADHD – thus treatment with stimulants was unethical. When dyslexia was diagnosed this was treated with remedial reading, without acknowledging problems of attention and behaviour. Co-ordination problems were often treated with an old-fashioned idea, sensory motor integration therapy. The associated problems of behaviour and school underfunction were again not even considered.

The correct treatment for a child does not have to be an either/or exercise. Two or more conditions can coexist and each must be taken seriously.

Specific learning disabilities (SLD)

Approximately 50 per cent of children with ADHD also suffer some specific weakness in learning. If a child is diagnosed with a specific learning disability this means that there is a significant discrepancy between their tested intelligence and their performance in certain specific areas. The most frequent discrepancies are in reading, spelling, writing, language and mathematics.

The child's ADHD does not cause the learning disabilities, though its presence makes remediation less successful. The treatment of ADHD with medication does not directly affect problems of learning, but medication can help the child to sit, settle, concentrate and be available to learn.

Parents are often unprepared for the slow, painful progress of treating a child with major dyslexia or Language Disorder. It is tempting to chase expensive and alternative cures in an attempt to speed things up. In the end most children with major reading problems do improve, but remain weak readers and spellers no matter how much pain we cause along the way.

We know that ADHD is a highly inheritable condition, and so too are most specific learning disabilities. The majority of children with a major reading problem have a close relative who reads and spells poorly. Parents whose children have a Language Disorder often say there is no family history of this, but when we try to unravel what the parents tell us, it seems that one of us has got a language problem.

Oppositional Defiant Disorder (ODD)

Oppositional Defiant Disorder is one of the most common comorbidities (it is claimed that 40 per cent of ADHD children are also ODD). ADHD children may be impulsive and unthinking, but following the event they are genuinely remorseful. This is not the case with ODD children, who may feel indignant and totally justified in the stand they took.

It is hard to know where oppositional behaviour starts – normal toddlers are negative, but pathological defiance is unusual before the preschool years. The spectrum of ODD varies from a mildly oppositional attitude to a constant state of hostile defiance.

The hostile ODD child is 'in your face' and seems to salute the world with a rude gesture. Children can have ODD without ADHD, but when ODD and ADHD combine this association of defiance and the explosive, unthinking behaviour creates a volatile mixture.

The origin of ODD seems to be largely biological (ie in the child's temperamental make-up) but the incidence and severity of the problem are greatly affected by parenting. *Parents who force, confront and are hostile in their relationships greatly increase the risk and extent of ODD in their children.*

There is no drug treatment for ODD. The management involves a slow behavioural approach which has limited success.

Now, before you give up in despair and slit your wrists, there is some good news. If ODD children survive to adulthood, their future is generally favourable. At home as

ODD children tend to say 'No' on principle. They wait for their parents to draw the line, so they can jump over it.

children and teenagers they seem to resent their parents, but in later life they mellow and most will regret the path they took – although by this time it may be too late.

Conduct Disorder (CD)

This is one comorbid behaviour that no parent wants to see. The media often wrongly diagnoses CD behaviour as ADHD.

The behaviours of conduct disorder (CD) include lying, cheating, stealing, threatening, cruelty, violating the rights of others, destruction of property, fire-setting and inflicting pain. It must be remembered that the unthinking ADHD child is quite capable of the occasional antisocial act, but after the event they understand what they have done and show remorse. Those with moderate or severe CD continue along the same path and show no moral regrets.

The incidence of CD in North America is close to 20 per cent, but we believe it to be somewhat less in Australia and New Zealand.

CD can occur in isolation, without being associated with ADHD, and in this form its onset is usually in adolescence. When CD is associated with ADHD it usually starts young, with a severe presentation of ODD before features of CD first come through between the age of seven and 10 years.

It is believed that the ADHD child who is free from CD at the age of 12 years is unlikely to develop the condition later on. This suggests there is a window of opportunity to change this catastrophic course, a child's future being won or lost in the early years. Though almost all ADHD children with CD also have severe features of ODD, the majority of children with ODD do not progress to develop CD.

The factors that increase the risk of CD are marital discord, hostile–critical parenting, and probably the poor early treatment of ADHD.

The treatment of CD requires the help of a clever and patient child's psychiatrist.

Depression

It is not uncommon for children or adults to be depressed, whether they have or do not have ADHD. Depression is rarely an issue before children start to compare and compete in primary school. ADHD children yearn to behave, learn and be accepted as others, just like their peers, but they simply don't know how to make this happen. It is normal for ADHD children to be disillusioned, but this does not make for a diagnosis of pathological depression.

The depressed child slips into a chronic state where they are moody, preoccupied, sad and wish to withdraw. Some put a brave face on things while others show their stress by becoming more irritable and annoying. The diagnosis is not easy to describe in words but parents should be concerned when they sense in their child a change of personality, a withdrawal from usual activities, a difficulty in close communication, a deeper state of sadness or notice a decline in schoolwork.

When depression and ADHD coexist, the depression should be treated as the first priority.

Tics and Tourette syndrome

Minor twitches and involuntary movements are common in the general population, but have a much higher incidence in those with ADHD. Tics refer to involuntary twitches, usually around the eyes or face, but sometimes a clearing of the throat, movement of the neck or shrug of a shoulder. The most extreme form of tic disorder, Tourette syndrome, involves throat noises, other major involuntary movements and occasionally the uttering of inappropriate words. Tics and Tourette are both comorbid conditions to ADHD.

The usual history of tics is to first appear when the child is around the age of seven to 10 years and to follow a course which comes and goes. As stimulant medication is first given around this age, it is easy to incorrectly believe that the drug has caused the tic.

Those who study tic disorder and Tourette syndrome state that the presence of tics rarely causes any significant problem in behaviour, learning or emotional well-being. The same cannot be said for the presence of ADHD which can cause great disadvantage in all these areas. When a child with a tic is said to underfunction, it is usually the coexisting ADHD, not the tic, that is causing the difficulty. This is important to understand when planning treatment. Tics and Tourette syndrome are no longer a contra-indication to the use of stimulant medication. If ADHD is causing big problems, it needs to be treated.

The clumsy child

Difficulties with co-ordination, motor planning, written work and late neurological maturity are all commonly associated with ADHD. When ADHD and comorbid clumsiness coexist, some therapists see only the motor problems, calling this 'the Clumsy Child Syndrome'. Their intentions are good, but the child is only half helped if the problems of learning and behaviour are misinterpreted.

The failure to see the association between ADHD and these comorbid conditions remains one of the most frequent causes of misunderstanding and incorrect treatment.

Finally, to add further confusion, these comorbid conditions are greatly influenced by the child's home and school environment. It would seem that the seeds that give the best and worst outcomes in ADHD are sown at a very early age. Environmental–parenting influences are now discussed in Chapter 7.

SEVEN

Parenting and ADHD

Twenty-five years ago most Australian and UK psychiatrists believed that bad behaviour was the result of family stress and poor parenting. When children presented with ADHD, all blame landed on the parents without any mention of biology, brain or the benefits of medication.

Over the years there has been a hard and often bloody battle fought to turn these out-of-date attitudes around. At the time of writing, all but a small cluster of 'psychodynamic dinosaurs' have seen the light. Modern research shows that ADHD is caused by a difference in brain function that can be successfully treated with medication.

The war may have been won, but the victory was achieved at a cost. In order to get the parent-blamers to listen, it was necessary to overstress the importance of biology and brain chemicals. Now that paediatricians, psychiatrists and parents are coexisting in peace, it's time to look at parenting in a more balanced way. Certainly ADHD is driven by brain chemicals, but parents are immensely influential in affecting the outcome.

Parents – the ways we damage our children

When we are given a difficult child there are two ways we can parent. We can accept, avoid escalation, support and nurture or we can make no concessions, criticise and apply ever-increasing force.

It requires immense patience to nurture the ADHD child but this brings benefits for esteem and ongoing relationships. It is much easier to force our expectations on children, but force results in resentment, hostility and a child who is angry with the world.

There is a message which keeps being repeated throughout this book: *it is best to accept and nurture.* With ADHD, the alternative just does not work.

Focus on failure

The problems that every adult meets in life are only as big as we choose to see them. A tired, defeated parent might see their ADHD child as 90 per cent disobedient, difficult and dumb, with only 10 per cent talent and charm. A stranger would be able to take a step back from the front line and see the exact opposite. When a parent is unhappy in their own life, unsupported and resentful, they often perceive their children as much worse than they really are. If we incorrectly think a child is 90 per cent difficult, our persistent put-downs may turn this perception into reality.

Depressed parents

Depression is common in many parents. If it is present, it is made worse by having an ADHD child, who in turn is more difficult through having a depressed parent. Depression does not cause ADHD, but helping a depressed parent brings great benefit to the child, and all the family.

A depressed mother will have so little emotional energy that those who depend on her will feel this flatness. With depression, problems – whether big or little – become blurred and seem equally immense. There is a feeling of numbness which makes us overreact to unimportant issues, or we may totally withdraw and react to nothing. The management of an ADHD child requires a resourceful, clear-thinking mind, and this is not available in depression.

Two million Australians (more than 10 per cent of the population) will be significantly depressed at some point in their lives.

The first step is to recognise these feelings, the second is to seek help. For most, the modern treatment of depression is simple and effective. Your GP is your first port of call.

ADHD in the parent

If management of ADHD is going to work, there must be structure, organisation, consistency and a parent who thinks before they act. The bad news is that ADHD is strongly hereditary and this frequently affects one parent. The good news is that the impulsive, disorganised parent is usually not the mother. Whether we like to admit it or not, mothers still provide the most structure and nurture in the homes of today's children.

If you are a parent with ADHD it is important to take a step back and see your vulnerabilities. Be obsessive about structure, routine, organisation and thinking before you blast the child with both barrels. We can't alter the attitude of our partner, but we can always smarten up our own act. See Chapter 16 for some practical suggestions to help you get started.

Family dysfunction

The evidence is inescapable: ADHD and CD are much more common where there is disharmony, dysfunction and a split family. The analytical psychiatrists claim ADHD behaviours are actually caused by these dysfunctions, but the truth is much more complex.

An ADHD child often inherits the disorder from a parent, and then the presence of that ADHD parent increases the risk of break-up and disharmony. The disharmony affects the family's stability and consistency, which in turn cause tension in the child's living environment. This increases the severity of the ADHD and damages the outcome for the child.

A common pattern for ADHD–CD men is to conceive, then leave. The mother is then stuck with the difficult child of a difficult man.

But not all disharmony is due to parents with ADHD. In Australia, New Zealand and the UK, almost one-third of all relationships will break up before our children have left school. This must represent an immense amount of dispute, disagreement and unhappiness in our homes.

There is no quick cure, but we must try to lessen the impact of fighting and parental disputes on all children, especially those with ADHD. Where possible, an amicable resolution to parent problems is always in the child's best interest. Anger with our partners may make us feel better but it does not suit children.

The mobile lifestyle

The genes of ADHD do predispose families to more restless, mobile, unsettled lifestyles. When I visit the remote mining towns of Australia I see many isolated mothers with challenging children. The busy menfolk love the 24-hour action of the mine – the mothers miss their friends, family and the support of grandparents.

Even in the cities our ADHD families are more mobile, with frequent changes of home and school. It may be a necessity of life, but mothers and children cope best with a stable, long-term place to live and, where possible, a close extended family.

We don't want to encourage a boring, entrenched lifestyle, but much of the moving about in ADHD adults is ill-considered and unhelpful. Itchy feet may be a part of ADHD, but shooting ourselves in the foot is no remedy.

Parents – the way we nurture our children

It's a bit one-eyed to see parents as the only players in influencing a child's emotional health. Many other people play a part: teachers, friends, in-laws, schoolmates – even the soccer coach. Despite this, when it comes to the crunch, parents are the majority shareholders and we have the greatest influence. Here are some suggestions to help grow your investment in your happy, healthy ADHD child.

Accept and adapt

ADHD is real; it's in the child's brain and in the short term the ADHD is not going to go away. Until this fact is accepted and allowances are made, you will get nowhere. Accepting and adapting our attitudes are the first steps in successful parenting.

Help your child to belong

I recently attended a wedding held by a wonderful, warm Greek family. The bride had one pageboy, her three-year-old nephew; a bundle of immense mischief and energy. At the reception he pulled off her veil, hid under her dress, slid round the dance floor, pushed over the flower girls and was into everything.

But this was no problem – everyone knew John, they diverted his excesses, protected his safety and lovingly smiled at his immense exuberance. This boy belonged; he knew he was loved, accepted and enjoyed by his family and their friends. This idea of belonging to an extended family or group of friends may seem old-fashioned and stuffy, but it is of immense importance to the emotional health of both adults and children, particularly those affected by ADHD.

Enlist a non-critical supporter

Children from one to eight years are closely dependent on their parents, while after this age others exert their influence. It seems that children are at their best emotionally if able to talk and confide with an accepting adult. This can be mum, dad, aunts, grandparents, a teacher or a friend. What they want is a supporter who believes in them.

A good grandparent can do more for an ADHD child than a whole convention full of counsellors.

A close grandparent can be a great ally. They are less rushed than parents and far enough from the front line of day-to-day discipline to be an impartial listener.

Make sure your child knows where they stand

It would be easy to misinterpret our non-confronting approach as letting children get away with murder. Certainly we are not looking for fights, but a few clearly stated and firmly followed through rules are essential.

Rules are not to be made in the heat of battle, they are laid down in a time of clear thought and calm. When a behaviour happens, the rule is stated, the repercussions are outlined, then calmly followed through without debate (see Chapter 10). All human beings are at their emotional best when they operate within clearly defined limits and ADHD children are no exception. They need to know exactly where they stand.

Remember the magic word: nurture

By this stage in the book our readers must be heavily overdosed on the word nurture. It keeps arising for a good reason – we believe it is vitally important. The child with ADHD can be immensely irritating, but most are sensitive and inwardly they wish to please. When they misbehave they don't need to be shot out of the water by the heavy artillery. Nice kids remain nice when accepted as they are, given realistic limits, guided, rewarded, enjoyed and loved.

They don't want to be managed by force or fear, they need a parent who is a supporter, a believer and a friend.

ADHD may be caused by an imbalance of brain chemicals, but the outcome is heavily influenced by us, the parents. We can meet fire with fire and escalate the situation to warlike proportions. This may give the superficial appearance of control, but compliance through fear wrecks relationships and robs children of love. Accepting, supporting, guiding, encouraging, rewarding and enjoying may seem like surrender, but when your child is at the age of 18 years, you will see we were right.

EIGHT

ADHD – Making the Diagnosis

There is no one black-and-white test for ADHD. Anyone who sees the diagnosis in such simple terms has read too many books and worked with far too few children.

If this were an ideal world, each child would have intensive work-ups by psychologists, educators, behaviouralists, occupational therapists, speech pathologists and a paediatrician. But the world we work in has such limited resources we must be economic in assessment and concentrate our energies on providing proper treatment and long-term support.

If parents are concerned with the possibility of ADHD, they should first discuss this with the child's teacher to discover if the child's behaviour is causing concern.

The authors of this book use different methods of assessment, based on their research and practical experience. When Kit Chee assesses, she uses formal questionnaires, detailed objective testing and a carefully taken history. Chris Green relies more on the subtleties of history, the presentation of the child and the reports of teachers. We believe that the children and parents in our care are equally well served by either of these approaches. It is the positive response to our intervention that is important, not the individual diagnostic method.

Diagnosis – the four steps

We see the diagnosis of ADHD as being comprised of four simple steps:

1. Look for alarm signals.

2. Exclude ADHD lookalikes.

3. Use some objective pointers towards diagnosis.

4. Take a detailed history tuned to the subtleties of ADHD.

1. Alarm signals

There are two main alarm signals that should always make one think of ADHD:

A. Significantly underfunctions at school

Most parents seek our help after the start of school. The teacher is bewildered as this child appears clever but is unable to deliver the goods. The teacher arranges for an educational psychologist (district school counsellor) to test overall intellect and to exclude specific learning disabilities. The results show a degree of failure which is not in keeping with the intellect and specific learning abilities. ADHD must now be considered.

B.   Unexpected behaviour problems

At home every child in this family has equal love and discipline, yet this child stands out as many times more difficult than the others. The parents will be making heavy weather of management, due to a cluster of tell-tale ADHD behaviours. This child is significantly out of step with his peers and siblings.

Once alerted to the possibility of ADHD, it is time to move to the next step.

2.   Exclude ADHD lookalikes

Many academic articles imply that ADHD is easily confused with a long list of lookalike behaviours. The most commonly quoted include:

The normal, active preschooler

The amount of activity, commonsense and intensity of behaviour varies greatly in preschoolers. Some normally active children are called overactive, but they do not have ADHD. Their problem is a busy temperament which conflicts with the sometimes unreasonable expectations of their parents.

To diagnose ADHD in a preschooler, the behaviours must be inappropriate even for this normally active and unthinking stage of development. This lookalike behaviour can be quite difficult to distinguish from ADHD, even for experts. When in doubt, we arrange a good preschool, give basic behaviour suggestions and see what happens over the next few months. Hopefully the diagnosis will then be clearer.

Intellectual disability

Parents often confuse their child's intellectual disability with ADHD. If you have a five year old with the development of a two-and-a-half year old, you must expect the behaviour to be active, inattentive and unthinking – but this is not ADHD.

Children with this developmental delay are also at increased risk of suffering from ADHD. When these two coexist, the behaviour must be significantly out of step with the intellectual level, otherwise the diagnosis cannot be considered. Stimulant medication can be used in children with intellectual disability, but it has less chance of success.

The hearing-impaired child

Children with severe hearing loss can present with atypical behaviour, but their behaviour is more unresponsive and distant than that of ADHD children. Inattentive children don't listen and are often sent for hearing tests. Frequently, they are found to have a mild hearing loss caused by fluid in the middle ear (glue ear). This minor reduction in hearing does not cause ADHD, but it makes life much harder for the already inattentive child.

If there is even the slightest doubt about any child's hearing, this must be formally tested.

Specific learning disabilities (SLD)

If children have a specific weakness in learning, such as dyslexia, they become frustrated and lose concentration when the work becomes too hard. In these children the inattention only occurs when they are struggling with reading, mathematics, language or whatever causes them stress. In ADHD the difficult behaviours and problems of persistence are present most of the time. However, as ADHD and specific learning disabilities (SLD) regularly coexist, it can sometimes be difficult to separate the behaviours of these two conditions.

3. Pointers towards diagnosis

Over the years researchers have worked hard to bring some science to the diagnosis of ADHD. A list of diagnostic criteria has been developed to help practitioners and questionnaires allow teachers and parents to rate the behaviours. Psychologists have developed tests and profiles that point to the presence of ADHD. Others have devised ways to measure attention and persistence. Recently, advanced electronics have allowed the analysis of brainwaves, which some believe to be helpful.

Professionals may promote their method of assessment as the one and only way, but there remains no completely reliable test for ADHD. The methods currently available bring some objectivity into a very subjective area, but they are not foolproof and should only be seen as pointers towards a probable diagnosis of ADHD.

The American Psychiatric Association have published guidelines for the diagnosis of ADHD which list nine possible behaviours of ADHD (the 'diagnostic criteria').

For a child to have ADHD, they need to show six out of the nine possible behaviours. If they demonstrate six or more, it is ADHD; five or less and the diagnosis is in dispute. This seems so clear-cut, but it is not.

The child with four or five difficult behaviours may not fit the full criteria, but can still cause immense stress. The child with six behaviours may not come for treatment if the parents are saints and the school superb. A child from a dysfunctional home and unsupportive school may only have five features and receive treatment.

This subjective movement of the goal posts annoys the academics. Their problem is they can only see what they read in books; we have to cope with the variables of real life.

4. Detailed history and observation

After seeing many ADHD children it becomes apparent that no two are exactly the same. Despite this, if one takes a careful history, there are usually telltale signs:

Frequent findings with ADHD children
Impulsive–hyperactive and combined subtypes

- Many became toddler tornadoes the moment they got up on their feet.

- There is a dramatic difference between the academic achievement in a one-to-one situation versus unsupervised study.

- At home most ADHD children are insatiable, go on and on, and generate immense tension.

  For many, the first school report used the words 'disruptive' and 'distractible'.

- Their behaviour in a group is often embarrassing and when playing with one other child they are overpowering and bossy.

- Their impulsivity makes them both verbally and physically accident-prone.

- In the doctor's office the younger, impulsive, over-active children are easy to diagnose. The moment these children walk in the door, the doctor will by reflex reach out to protect their property.

- Older children present less dramatically. Most, but not all, squirm, fidget and fiddle. Their talk often gets sidetracked or they become lost in mid-sentence. Asking questions often gets the answer, 'Good'. Their eyes and minds are all over the place.

  We estimate that more than 90 per cent of ADHD children can be identified by a properly tuned history.

- Sometimes ADHD will not be obvious in the doctor's office

and then the diagnosis is made by listening carefully to the parents. When this happens, ADHD is diagnosed in the same way as many other medical conditions, for example, epilepsy; that is, by history. Doctors don't ask to see the epileptic fall to the floor and fit in front of them, they believe what parents tell them.

Predominantly inattentive subtype

- There is a dramatic difference between the academic achievement in a one-to-one situation versus unsupervised study.

- These children are disorganised, forgetful and drift effortlessly off task.

- Those who present with pure inattention and subtle problems of learning are much more difficult to diagnose, and with them the tests and pointers are of special value.

If two months down the track a young life has had a major turnaround, we probably got it right!

- When it all seems too difficult, remember that we diagnose for one reason – so that we can help.

Making the diagnosis: three plans for assessment

As we hear some colleagues talk about ADHD and specific learning disabilities (SLD), it seems that the diagnosis is impossible without a team of psychologists and a month of time. Resources are so limited at present, anyone who teaches about ADHD must be clear as to what are the essentials for diagnosis and what are the impractical academic ideals.

With this in mind we put forward our three plans for assessment: the basic, the more objective and the comprehensive. The quality of local resources, and the size of your wallet, will decide which you choose.

Diagnosis is only the start; it is what happens after that which really matters.

1. The basic method

Be alerted

- Behaviour out of step with parenting (fidgets, impulsive, insatiable, socially out of tune).
- Underfunctions at school (disruptive, distractible, inattentive, poor memory, needs one-to-one supervision).

Exclude

- Obvious intellectual disability.

- Major family dysfunction.

Talk to school

- Is there any worry re intelligence?

- Is there any worry re SLD?

- What are the school's concerns?

Appointment with

- School psychologist, paediatrician or child psychiatrist. These professionals will make the diagnosis having considered the above, which is then confirmed by parents' description and clinical presentation in the office.

Trial of stimulants

Monitored by:

- Feedback from school.

- Feedback from parents.

2. The more objective method

Same as basic method, but add:

Paperwork

- Questionnaires completed by parents.
- Questionnaires completed by school.
- Formal report from school/preschool.

Educational psychologist (school counsellor)

- Basic tests of intellect.
- Screening tests for SLD.
- Classroom visit to observe.

3. The more comprehensive method

Same as more objective method, but also add:

Specialised tests

- Psychologist: detailed tests of general abilities (such as WISC-IV) and specific areas of learning.
- Educationalist: practical assessment of basic abilities in classroom learning.

- Paediatrician–Psychologist: Paired Associate Learning Test; Continuous Performance Type Test; QEEG (eg Neurometrics).

Trial of stimulants

Monitored by some of the following:

- Questionnaires.
- Paired Associate Learning Test.
- QEEG.
- Continuous Performance Test.
- Feedback from school.
- Feedback from parents.

NINE

The Stresses on Parents and Siblings

The difficulties experienced with ADHD are not the same for every family. These depend on the severity of the ADHD, whether the main features are behaviour or learning problems, and the presence or absence of comorbid conditions such as Oppositional Defiant Disorder. These children cause immense stress both to their parents and their siblings.

It would be safe to assume that a house charged with ADHD energy would not be a quiet place to relax.

Stress-damaged parents

The number of experts who have to see a child before the correct diagnosis is made never ceases to amaze. Recently we saw an eight year old with classic ADHD. Over the previous two years the parents had sought help from one private and two school psychologists, an occupational therapist, a paediatrician and two different child psychiatrists. An impressive list of learning, co-ordination and emotional diagnoses had been made but none of them included ADHD. As this busy boy bounced into our waiting room, an elderly grandmother looked up and said, 'He's got ADHD just like my grandson'. She was right. It's a strange world where an insightful grandparent can see much more clearly than a college full of professionals.

It's my fault

As parents of ADHD children look at their friends, it seems they all have angelic, compliant children. With ADHD even the most knowledgeable, best-balanced parent will secretly believe that they are in some way to blame. This feeling is made worse by out-of-date community attitudes and the ignorant prejudices of powerful people in the media.

Then there are those interfering friends who question the diagnosis and tell the parents that the treatment is not safe. We know these children are difficult, but they would be many times worse if it weren't for their exceptional parents.

It upsets us to see good mums and dads blame themselves.

Disappointment, resentment, anger

By the time we see families the parents have done their best, but nothing they try seems to work. This leaves them feeling impotent and inadequate. Many are secretly disappointed that parenting has not lived up to expectations. Others are angry that one child has brought so much stress and disruption to what was once a hassle-free home.

Some mothers have supportive, heavily involved husbands and a good extended family, others carry all the worry and childcare themselves. Many look to us to work some miracle – they can't believe life was meant to be this difficult.

Dads appear better than mums

In most households it is still the mother who provides 90 per cent of the care and parenting. But despite this, many fathers seem more in control than the mums. It is not that mothers are poor parents, it's just that fathers tend to be firmer, louder and make a greater impact as they are less often at home.

Children cause poor parenting

The parents we see start out with such high ideals, but after years of hitting their heads against a brick wall they pull back on their discipline and go for the easier path. A professional, who knows nothing of their early struggle, sees the bad behaviour and blames it on the apparent lack of firmness. *They do not realise that discipline has moved this way as a result of the difficulty faced by the parents.*

A group of researchers used video recordings to assess the quality of discipline. When the videos were analysed, the parents of ADHD children did not rate well. They were snappy, stressed, negative and often inconsistent. On face value this proved that poor parenting caused the ADHD children to behave badly.

These children were then given their stimulant medication and refilmed. With the calmness brought to their child by medication, the parents were found to be in control and disciplining well. The parents were as competent as any other parents – it was the children who had changed. Many childcare experts have not yet grasped this fact. It is the behaviour of an ADHD child that makes good parents appear poor, not poor parenting that creates the behaviour of ADHD.

Some parents can't be helped

There is another side to this: some parents refuse to accept the nature of ADHD. As we talk they won't listen – they won't change and can't be helped. Usually there are three issues involved:

Treat all equally

Some mothers and fathers are quite angry when we suggest they treat the ADHD child in a different way to their siblings. 'He's not going to change our life', 'You can't tell us that one child should be treated differently', 'If they are going to live in our house they will live by the same rules'. With this attitude these parents make no allowances for ADHD – and so the child is always in trouble, home is unhappy and this constant criticism erodes their esteem.

Looking for trouble

A country mother recently complained that the trip home from school was a time of great tension: 'I stop to get the groceries, when I return to the car he has his brothers and sisters at each other's throats'. We suggested she do her shopping on the way to pick up the children but this minor change in routine would not be considered.

Beat it out of them

If the child had a more obvious disability, it would be easier to accept. If they had been born with only one leg we would not force them to run. If they were deaf we would accept that no amount of shouting or beating would make them hear. Some parents refuse to recognise that ADHD is a genuine physical condition, then push, punish and get nowhere.

Some fathers are just as uninsightful, inflexible and impulsive as the children they produced: 'I would never have been allowed to get away with this when I was a boy, I'll knock it out of him'. This heavy approach may achieve the impression of compliance, but don't be fooled.

There must be supermen and wonderwomen out there who find ADHD easy, but so far we have not met them. *The parents we deal with are tired, confused and frequently full of self-doubts.* Many have already had a real run-around. Often they have been told: 'There's nothing wrong', 'It's poor parenting', 'You need to be stricter', 'Have you thought of a Parent Effectiveness Course?'.

Obedience through fear robs the relationship of love and respect.

Siblings also suffer

I am sure some siblings wish they had been born an only child or possibly adopted out at birth. Despite this most brothers and sisters adapt, learning how to steer around explosions and avoid catching their brother's blame. There are a number of reasons for brothers and sisters to call this unfair:

Different rules for different people

'But Mum, you would never let *me* get away with that.' We hear this all the time, but if we don't have different rules and expectations, home will become a front-line war zone. Siblings must be told that their brother is a *clever creative kid, but he's lost the lever that applies the brakes to behaviour*. It's unfair, but whether you like it or not there are going to be different rules.

Invasion of space

'It's not fair Mum, he's breaking my toys.' Many ADHD children have fiddly fingers, an inquisitive mind and no strong views on ownership. If you are going to live together for the next 10 years there must be some firm rules about what can and cannot be touched: 'Your brother's bedroom has been declared a total no-go area.' 'Upsetting your sister's homework will never be allowed.' 'If you as much as tap on her door or put your nose inside, a bolt of lightning will descend!' Older brothers and sisters need their space, particularly when coming close to exam times. A door lock is not an unreasonable solution.

Taunts and tension

'Mum, he won't leave me alone!' Siblings talk, play and watch the TV together, but the ADHD child intrudes like a fully charged detonator. They poke, tease, insult and go on until even the cat and goldfish need therapy. Of course the siblings themselves are not without guilt. Some rise to great heights in their ability to stir up their brother with ADHD. This keeps the house in a constant state of red alert.

Parents must notice and praise when everyone is getting on together. If the conflict is plummeting out of control, it's time to separate the warring parties.

In some families, nothing short of a general anaesthetic will bring peaceful coexistence.

Siblings and school

'Do you know what your brother did in class today?' It's tough enough having a brother or sister who is 'full on', but their school behaviours are not your problem. Siblings must be taught to smile and side-step such comments, but they still hurt.

Ruined for all of us

'Mum, it's not our fault, why do we have to go home early?' With any difficult child there must be limits to outside family activities. It's not fair for brothers and sisters but we can make it up to them. We may not always be able to do things as a family, but one parent can watch the sibling's soccer game, and take part in activities that would be impossible if the ADHD child was present.

Friends fed up

'Mum, he's annoying my friend!' When friends come around to play there may be bossing, teasing, interfering or hijacking the brother's or sister's friend for themselves. As social skills in ADHD are often weak, it's important to encourage the visits. Before the event set down some clear rules about what you expect and what you don't want. Give feedback when they play well, separate when they squabble, and keep ever-vigilant.

An uneven distribution of time

'Mum, you spend all your time doing things with John.' An ADHD child consumes an immense amount of time and nervous energy. There are visits to doctors, therapists and tutors, supervision of homework and constantly keeping a lid on behaviour. Certainly the distribution of time is unfair, but it's unavoidable. To allow the

How to protect siblings

- Have a few non-negotiable rules about brother's and sister's space and property.

- Provide some secure places for storage.

- Make a rule that damage to others' property is repaired by a levy from pocket money.

- Enforce an absolute veto on any disturbance to homework or study.

- Allow older brothers and sisters to have a lock on their bedroom door.

- Separate squabbling siblings into different rooms.

- Have realistic limits on family excursions.

- Allocate one parent to be fully available for events such as the sibling's Saturday sport.

- Arrange overnight stays with family and friends, to share care.

maximum amount of time with the siblings make use of all resources including fathers, grandparents and friends.

No one said life was going to be easy. Even though parents feel guilty and siblings simmer, most families manage and still remain close. I recently reviewed a difficult boy whose teenage sisters wanted to attend the interview. They complained to their mum: 'You don't tell Dr Green the truth. The doctor doesn't know that our brother John is such a prize pain'. We don't need a band of placard-waving siblings to protest outside our offices, we know how it feels.

TEN

The Top Tips for
Better Behaviour

This chapter looks at the basic building blocks of better behaviour in children with ADHD. Though the same techniques may be used with oppositional children, they are much less effective. Before we go any further it must be clearly stated that applying behaviour techniques alone will not produce miracles. We must first refocus the severe ADHD child using medication. *You have to reach before you can teach.*

Why usual methods fail

The techniques we use so successfully with other children don't work well in ADHD. For a behaviour program to be effective, a child first needs to listen, plan ahead, remember, consider before they act and be motivated by rewards. These are the weaknesses of ADHD, which explains why these children are so difficult to discipline. The ADHD child hears half the instruction and then forgets the rest. They don't see the sequence of events that is leading them into trouble, where action A leads to B, to C – and by E they are sliding into disaster.

The modern understanding of ADHD recognises a weakness of frontal lobe function which causes poor control of unwise behaviour. In ADHD, an idea hits the front of the mind and the child acts without thinking of the repercussions.

If lack of impulse control derails discipline, the situation is made worse by a poor response to reinforcement and reward. The average child will tidy their toys, be rewarded with a chocolate biscuit, smile and do it again. The ADHD child gets the biscuit, complains it is not Belgian chocolate with speckles, then nags for another then another. These problems of planning ahead, acting without proper thought and responding poorly to rewards make ADHD behaviour hard to manage.

Steps in behaviour management

When you follow parents through the ups and downs of many years, it seems some of our suggestions work and others are a waste of time. The best results come with clear communication, simple instructions, a small number of important rules, and rewards which are regular and repeated.

Most parents turn the corner when they realise it is preferable to back off and not go for the jugular over every trivial irritation. For many the miracle came with the introduction of medication which gave them a child who thought, listened and was *easier to reach*. All parents feel stronger when they understand ADHD and realise they are not alone. But let's look at the full list of techniques that help produce better behaviour.

Routine, structure, consistency

As human beings we are all happier when life is predictable and we know where we stand. This need for structure is many times more important in the ADHD child, who likes to have a fixed framework to direct their day. They wake at a certain time, put their pyjamas under their pillow, straighten the doona, get dressed, have breakfast, brush their teeth, feed the goldfish and leave for school. If their equilibrium is thrown by anything different – a late night, a relief teacher, visitors to the classroom or a school excursion – this will set them off.

If you want peace, keep to routine.

Get their attention

Whether you are training elephants in the circus, toddlers or a child with ADHD, nothing will happen until you get their attention. Speak clearly, directly and address them by name. The secret to communication is eye contact, simple words, enthusiasm and step-by-step instructions.

Ignore the unimportant

If they blow a raspberry, slurp their drink or a pea falls to the floor, does it really matter? Successful parents realise the importance of taking a step back and only engaging in the big battles.

With wriggly young children, hold their hands or direct their face towards yours. *Briefly* touch older children to gain attention.

Avoid escalation

Some parents get so heated in their reaction they escalate every unimportant behaviour. We know it can be irritating, but don't add fuel to the fire. Try to stay calm, use a matter-of-fact voice and repeat the rule like a broken record.

Know what triggers behaviour

There are certain devastating events which are dynamite to discipline: children's parties, late nights, sickness, visitors, long car journeys, staying with relatives and any change of routine. It's not always possible to avoid these, but anticipating does makes it easier to handle.

In-between times

Most ADHD children cope with the structure of the classroom and the hype of the playground, but they can't handle the gap between. They hit the playground like an animal just released from captivity and if trouble comes it is often in the first five minutes. When they return to class they are the last to calm, settle and concentrate. Parents and teachers should know of this vulnerability and be on their guard in these 'in-between times'.

Medication increases focus

It's no secret that the authors of this book strongly support the use of stimulant medication in ADHD. Without it, the impulsive actions, lack of listening, and general disorganisation of ADHD will sabotage the best behavioural program. Medication allows the child to self-monitor, plan their response and be reached by reason. For most behavioural therapists, *it is medication that turns a good program into one that is brilliant.*

Too tough? Not tough enough?

We are strong believers in a gentle approach to ADHD, though at times we wonder if we are too permissive. On one hand we see parents who are uncompromising and tough, who have oppositional, resentful children. On the other are parents who are permissive and peace loving, who usually remain close to their less well behaved children. We don't know the correct formula, but there must be some rules and firmness. *Maybe the answer is 90 per cent nurture and 10 per cent toughness!*

Children need rules

We don't want to run our homes like the public service, every action governed by a hundred regulations, but there is room for a small, sensible framework of rules. These need to be drawn up in advance, created at a time of calm, not made in the heat of battle. They need to be simple, fair, few in number and clearly understood.

When a rule is challenged, it must be clearly restated and then enforced.

Avoid arguments

When they make arguing an Olympic sport, ADHD children will scoop all the medals. Arguing and debating with an ADHD child is a pointless pursuit – they are all words and no logic. Don't debate; you will never win and it shortens your life. State the rule and stand your ground.

The magic of 'One, Two, Three'

When confronted, most ADHD children refuse on principle. We tell them 'Do it now' and they look at us as if we were impaired.

Your grandmother had none of these problems, she asked politely and if there was no sign of action, quietly counted to three. Counting is a well tried, old technique, that gives that little bit of space needed to avoid reflex refusal.

Separate the warring parties – time out

You can have your rules and your counting techniques, but there comes a point where things are heading seriously out of control. Once behaviour gets past a certain point, there is no place for reason – now you must back off and get some space.

Time out allows a deteriorating situation to be salvaged by briefly removing the child from all attention and audience. The time period is approximately one minute for every year of life. With care, the technique can be used right up to the early teens.

When the time has been served, even though they are not openly repentant, they return to the real world. For time out to work it must be put in place without anger or debate, there must be no response to calling out and once it's finished they restart with a completely clean slate.

Successful discipline

■ All the effective behavioural treatments for ADHD involve living by routine, rewarding the good and taking a step back from confrontation.

■ Don't lock horns with an ADHD child and then increase the pressure. This produces a battle of wills, two angry parties, opposition, resentment and damage to relationships.

■ Don't argue. Don't get heated. Don't escalate. Use a matter-of-fact, unemotional, controlled voice.

■ Give yourself room to manoeuvre:
  • State the rule.
  • Count to three.
  • Use time out.
  • Give choices.
  • Don't force them into a cul-de-sac.

- Remember, even the worst behaved child is good 95 per cent of the time. Reward this positive side: catch them being good!

- In boxing, the victor is the one who uses most force. In parenting, the winner is the one whose children still love them at the age of 18 years.

Encouraging good behaviour with rewards

The basic law of behaviour modification states: 'A behaviour which pays off for the child will be repeated; a behaviour that brings no advantage to the child will disappear'. This means if we reward the right behaviour, it should happen more frequently, while ignoring what's undesired means it should go away.

To encourage the best behaviour we can use hard, soft or cumulative rewards. A hard reward is something tangible such as money, food or a special privilege. Soft rewards are praise, enthusiasm or a show of parental pride. Cumulative rewards refers to the collection of stars, stamps or tokens, each given for a small period of good behaviour and eventually adding up to a major prize.

Hard and soft rewards lose their effect unless they are specific and regularly repeated. When a reward is used long term, the pay-off must vary as this element of change prevents loss of interest or an increase in demands. Some ADHD behaviours respond best to ongoing rewards and for them we motivate with tokens and stars.

In the older ADHD child, privileges are an excellent form of motivation. A good burst of behaviour might be recognised by a later bedtime, choosing dinner, ordering a take-away, having a friend over to stay or being excused a usual household chore.

Once we start taking away privileges we are moving from the positive part of discipline into the realms of punishment. For privilege withdrawal to be effective, the privilege must be something the child depends on for pleasure. The usual loss of privilege involves missing half a favourite television program, no telephone tonight or the bicycle locked up until the weekend. To be effective, keep it short, don't enter any debate and choose something meaningful.

Punishment

Punishment must be treated with immense care as it is easy to get in much deeper than we wish. It is a valuable technique which helps defuse the short-term crisis and avoids escalation. Children are confused when an unexpected punishment arrives out of the blue. Others misinterpret the sequence of events and only see their father's anger: 'My Dad went psycho and I was grounded for a week'.

Smacking

It is politically incorrect to condone the slightest smack, but in the real world it still happens. The main dangers of smacking are escalation and resentment. You smack; the child looks defiant; you smack harder; they thumb their nose at you – and soon you are out of control. The more force you use, the more resentful they become.

Guidelines for punishment

- Use punishment sparingly.
- Give a clear warning.
- Think before you act.
- Communicate calmly.
- Have a clear beginning and end.
- Don't escalate.
- Once finished, let the matter drop.

Resentment and hate do not make for happy relationships.

We can't totally ban physical punishment but in ADHD it escalates, is ineffective, wrecks relationships and can be downright dangerous.

'I' statements – 'you' statements

It is possible to say the same thing in two ways, each getting a different response. If I use an 'I' statement, it transmits how 'I' feel. If I use a 'You' statement, it implies that 'You' are being criticised. When an ADHD child annoys us it is the behaviour we dislike, not the child. It may seem a trivial change, but where possible move from 'You' to 'I'. For example:

'You are always hurting your sister' becomes 'I get upset when there's so much fighting'. 'You've ruined the outing for all of us' becomes 'I am upset when we all have to come home early'.

On a bad day it may seem that nothing is going right, but even the worst child is in fact good 95 per cent of the time. The secret of successful discipline is to notice, reinforce and reward the good.

Discipline is a delicate balance of firmness and encouragement. It is not possible to overencourage, but it is easy to be too negative. When in doubt, take the peaceful path: hold out the olive branch of nurture, not the stick of punishment. Don't get demoralised: if managing ADHD was easy there would be no need for this book.

ELEVEN

Solving Common Behaviour Problems

It would be an insult to parents to pretend that the lists in this chapter will miraculously cure all behaviour problems. The suggestions are **Aim for peace, not perfection.** given for only one reason: to guide you in the right direction. Our aim is to give some simple pointers. Once you are standing at the battle front you will have to modify them as the events unfold.

Pokes and teases his sister at mealtimes

Have a few non-negotiable rules and let the rest pass:

- 'You can rabbit on about any topic but you can't tease, insult or abuse your sister.'

- 'You can wriggle, swing and touch but there must be absolutely no contact with your sister or anything she owns.'

- If the rule is broken, there is one warning, then action.

Slow to get ready for school

There are two sorts of slow starters, those who switch off (dreamers or 'spacers') and those who are out to annoy (foot draggers).

Dreamers

- With dreamy children, pack their school bag the night before and set out their clothes in preparation.

- Keep reminding, checking and encouraging progress.

- Reward results, don't get angry, don't despair.

Foot draggers

- Foot draggers need to know the rules.

- There is one wake-up call, a five-minute reminder, then a statement when it is 10 minutes before the school bus departs.

- Set a cooking timer which gives a warning. This avoids nagging.

- Eating breakfast on the run is unsatisfactory but it's better than conflict.

Don't allow a dawdling child to ruin the rest of your day.

- If they choose to be late, don't break the speed limits getting them there.

Interrupts like a preschooler

ADHD children are impulsive and forget if they don't tell you immediately. We must not block communication, but we should encourage them to wait.

- Give a gentle reminder: 'Your turn in a minute, John'.

- Keep repeating the rules of conversation, but don't become a negative nag.

- Allow the forgetful child to interrupt with a 'cue word', which you pick up later.

Surviving long car journeys

If you must drive:

When long-distance travel ages parents and is a hazard to mental health, consider a quick air flight, a seat on a train or simply stay home.

- Set down a few firm rules about teasing, poking and annoying, in advance.

- Plan regular breaks, and inform them of the travel time.

- If the car tape-player is to be used, allocate tape time in advance. An individual Walkman may help.

- Use a token system where short periods of peaceful travel are rewarded with a small token (a tick, star, bead, etc), which all adds up to a worthwhile reward (for example bonus spending money at the next stop).

Bad language – bad attitude

A child who is impulsive and socially immature can be rude and inappropriate in what they say. Oppositional children are often hostile.

- Words are often said for the reaction they get. Don't rise to the bait, make a clear statement that this is unacceptable, don't escalate or debate.

- In young children, explain the meaning of rude words and show the silliness of describing reproductive anatomy in public.

- There is a difference between a five year old who copies without thought and the entrenched bad language of a 15 year old. You can enforce some house rules in the adolescent, but the time to establish attitudes and language is much earlier on.

- Notice and reinforce when they talk, relate and respect in an appropriate way.

- Children parrot the speech, abusive attitudes and bad language of those they are close to. In the pre-school years this comes from us, the parents.

The bedroom is a mess

Order-loving mothers don't cope with a bomb blast bedroom. The best chance of tidiness comes when parents start young.

- Regularly cull all excess junk, toys and outgrown clothes.

- Provide easy-access storage and hanging space.

- With the young child, tidy the room together.

- Use the 'carrot' incentive: 'You tidy this and I'll get your drink ready'.

Is it worth driving a messy teenager out of your home for the sake of a clean bedroom?

- Have a pre-set inspection time each day.

- A star chart helps focus attention on the clean room but it loses effect within a few weeks.

- For each day of relative tidiness, add a small productivity bonus to the pocket money.

Breaks his sister's property

If you have an inquisitive mind, fiddly fingers and don't think ahead, things will get broken.

- Have a small number of rules about what can and what cannot be touched.

- Notice when they show care and respect for other people's property.

- Distinguish between the occasional unthinking act and damage which follows deliberately disregarding a warning.

- Instruct siblings to keep their treasures secure and make this a no-go area for their ADHD brothers.

- Breakages can be replaced using a small levy on the pocket money, which is deducted at source. Don't set up an impossibly harsh repayment system as this causes resentment and hostility.

Breaks in unthinking rage

The hyperactive, impulsive child can have a remarkably short fuse. When things go badly they overreact, even destroying their own treasures. After it's happened they see their stupidity, which makes them twice as upset.

Don't rub salt in the wound – even if they say they don't care, they are hurting.

- The angriest human beings are those who are angry at their own silliness.

- Don't nag as this adds insult to injury.

- If they break something important to them – for example an almost completed model aeroplane – support, don't criticise.

Lies – bending the truth

There is a difference between the occasional untruth of the young and the pathological planned deceit of an out-of-control adolescent.

- In the younger child, don't overreact, calmly say that you do not think it is true.

It is unfair to expect our children to be more truthful than the adults they live with.

- Don't debate, quietly state your opinion.

- Make sure that honesty pays off – they should receive less punishment for owning up than for denying fault.

- If you encourage openness when they are young, they should still confide in you in their tempestuous teens.

Dangerous bike riding

A bicycle gives a great outlet for the pent-up energy of the ADHD child. Unfortunately hyperactive, impulsive children can be a danger on the roads so we have to keep them safe.

- Have clear rules about helmets, stopping at intersections, crossing main roads and what areas are off-limits.

- Have rules about care of the bike, locking and putting it away at night.

- Notice and reinforce safe riding.

- Maintain some supervision when they are challenging their friends on jumps, ramps and riding through the air.

- When rules are disregarded, lock up the bicycle for a week and don't debate or argue your actions.

If you think bicycles are a worry, wait until they start driving your car!

Birthday parties

Often the hype and energy of so many children can still send the busy child ballistic.

- Prepare properly and arrive unstressed.

- Ensure medication has been given and will be in balance during the party hours.

- If worried about behaviour, go a little late and pick up early.

- With younger children, stay and help supervise.

- When organising your own child's party ensure you have enough adult minders on hand.

- Think of inviting a favourite teacher from school, as this provides a form of 'police presence'.

Socially out of tune

Some ADHD children push in, overpower, invade space, and the more they try, the worse it gets.

- Reinforce when they play well and interact appropriately.

- Give a brief reminder when their actions are upsetting others.

- Don't become negative or constantly criticise.

- Discreetly ask them how it would feel if they were in the other person's place.

- Social skills training programs seem essential for every ADHD child, but the results appear more successful in the therapy room than in the outside world.

- The development of social skills comes gradually with age and maturity.

Homework hassles

The secret is to get it right in the early school years: establish the homework habit and be an involved parent.

- Have a fixed homework time which allows some freedom to relax after school but is not late evening, when they are overtired.

- Have a special homework place.

- Have a contract which allocates a certain amount of full-focus work, followed by a break, then another period of work.

- If after an appropriate amount of effort the work is still unfinished, leave it there.

- Use reminders to make sure the right books come home and the requirements are understood.

- With school projects and high school study, parents still need to be involved, particularly to get them started.

TWELVE

Improving School Performance

Trying to teach an impulsive, inattentive child is never easy. Even with the best intervention available they will always have more talent and creativity than they are able to demonstrate in the examination hall. There are no simple solutions, but most success comes with teaching in small steps, and with variety, structure and tricks to help short-term memory.

Practical classroom suggestions
Which class?

The ADHD child thrives on calm, consistency and one-to-one encouragement. If they were royalty they would have a full-time personal tutor, but in the real world they will be taught in the same room as 30 others. When choosing a class, aim for the traditional closed-plan style.

Avoid the composite classes where more than one year's grade are taught together – unless there is some exceptional drawcard, such as a high teacher-to-pupil ratio.

ADHD children do not cope with disruption and must be protected from teachers with an unreliable attendance record or those planning long-service leave. In small schools, the challenging children are often placed in the class taken by the school principal. This may be the most tolerant and experienced teacher in school, but the ADHD child is unsettled by all the administrative interruptions. Even if placed in a sound-proof cell, these children are still capable of distracting themselves.

Choosing the right teacher

For the ADHD child, success at school varies greatly from year to year. It is not that these children change, it is just that some years the pupil and teacher hit it off and some years they don't.

All human beings like to be welcomed each day with enthusiasm and eye contact. We listen best to animated people who vary their voice and make each individual feel they are the one that matters. The ADHD child needs to know they are accepted and appreciated, but at the same time the teacher is definitely in charge.

The ideal teacher is firm, flexible and knows when to back off.

Sensible seating

It is tempting to hide the disruptive child as far away from the rest of the class as possible. But if they are going to learn the child needs to be near the front, preferably sandwiched between their two most placid classmates. They should be facing the teacher, looking at them eye to eye. Instructions should be given from in front of the child as they can lose direction when twisting to the side or back. Some companies who specialise in the training of business executives believe the U-shape seating plan gives best results, though space and department policy may not make this an option.

Order and organisation

The ADHD child needs to learn how to prioritise and organise or they will always underachieve. Teachers as well as parents can help this with rules, routine, lists and structure.

Rules

There should be a small number of clearly stated rules and regular reminders. At the start of each school day the rules about calling out in class, disturbing others and leaving your seat, are mentioned to all students. Special rules for the ADHD child are discussed with them in private.

Routine

They must know the plan at the start of each school day and be aware of what is going to happen next. When moving from one activity to another they need to be allowed to wind down, then must be picked up again on the other side.

The ADHD child must know what is expected and where they stand.

Lists

These are the life-savers for older children and adults. They list jobs for the day, homework and the equipment they need. Ticking off the completed tasks provides structure and gives a feeling of achievement.

Structure

- Planning and self-monitoring: Some time after the age of eight years, children can be taught to check and plan. At bedtime they are encouraged to consider the next day's activities, get their books ready, pack their sports clothes and think ahead.

- Teaching about sequence: We need to help ADHD children to organise their thoughts. The young child rushes in with some unintelligible story about a dog. Slow them down and say 'What dog?', 'Where was the dog?', 'What did the dog do?'. When reading a story stop at the end of a page and ask, 'What is going to happen next?'.

■ Self-talk: Bomb-disposal experts are more reliable when they talk themselves through the correct sequence of cutting the wires. Pilots run through a checklist prior to take-off. Talking aloud is not welcomed by teachers, but for some teenagers and adults it greatly improves accuracy.

■ A framework: When a child is forgetful and disorganised they need to work from a framework. 'What is the topic of this project?' 'What are the major headings?' 'What order do they come in?'

■ Time allocation: ADHD children have difficulty managing time. In an exam they allocate half the time to a quarter of the questions. When doing homework they spend an hour colouring a picture and leave little time for the writing. From the primary school years on, prioritising and time allocation are techniques that must be taught.

Holding attention

The greatest challenge for any teacher is to hold the ADHD child's attention without humiliating them in front of their mates. Attention is held with cue words, enthusiasm, variety, and with brief, step-by-step instructions.

Cue words

When the class is drifting the clever teacher uses words such as 'ready', 'wait for it', 'this is the interesting bit', 'now, here we go!'

Animated – enthusiastic

If teaching is presented in a bored, unexcited voice, the message is unlikely to get past the left earlobe. The animated teacher uses body language and their eyes, and pauses or talks softly to draw the children in.

Variety

Boredom is a big problem in ADHD and variation helps this loss of interest. Clever teachers change their tone of voice and the speed of presentation, or stop unexpectedly, all helping to reinforce listening.

Be brief

Instructions need to be short and to the point. Don't hide important messages in a mass of unnecessary words. Tell the child what you wish them to do, not what you do not want them to do.

Step-by-step instructions

Long lists of instructions do not suit the ADHD child. They have memory lapses, and forget the order, and this results in a shambles. In the early school years work should be presented in a series of simple steps. 'Take a clean page of paper.' 'Now take your ruler.' 'Put the ruler on the lefthand side.' 'Draw a line down the page.' 'Now take your pen . . .'

Improving memory

Those who live with an ADHD child or adult cannot believe how they forget so quickly. But we can improve memory using all sorts of cues, lists and memory jogs.

Visual cues

Verbal information is often lost, but when verbal is tagged to a visual cue, it may be held. In the early school years we learn our alphabet with an 'a' beside the picture of an 'apple'. Visual cues are not confined to school – we may not remember the floor in the carpark but we know it was the yellow level.

Key words and lists

Key words are used to draw the child's attention to an idea, in the hope it will jog their memory. Every mother uses this – her notes say 'milk', 'meat', 'pay bill'.

Association

When we are introduced to a group of people the names may be easier to remember if tagged to another image, for example Wendy – 'Peter Pan's friend', Kylie – 'the singer'.

Rhymes and mnemonics

As adults we remember '30 days has September, April, June and November'. We know 'i' before 'e' except after 'c'. The colours of the rainbow are red, orange, yellow, green, blue, indigo, violet: 'ROYGBIV'. If confused about whether to use 'principle' or 'principal', we remember it is 'our "pal" the principal'.

Memory jogs

Children can use the reminders that keep forgetful adults on track: writing on a hand, notes on a scrap of paper, knots in a handkerchief, an elastic band around the wrist, a watch on the wrong arm. Then there are gadgets such as a watch alarm, an electronic organiser and memo takers.

School behaviour

We understand how hard it is for parents at home with their ADHD child, but also how difficult it is for a teacher with these children amongst 30 others. Those who teach

ADHD children don't need a crystal ball to predict the problem areas. These children call out in class, touch and tap, overreact to teasing and don't cope with changes.

Calling out in class

This is part of their impulsive, immature, 'poor brakes' behaviour. They will never be the easiest child in the class, but there are some ways to help.

- Firstly, if the child is on medication ensure the levels are correctly balanced, as impulsive incidents increase when drugs drop off.

- These children must be cautioned for their call-outs, but not ridiculed in front of their mates.

- The whole class must be constantly reminded of the rules. For example, when this behaviour occurs the teacher makes a clear signal by using strong eye contact ('the look'), a special word or secret gesture. Tokens can be given for each 10 to 20 minutes of self-control, which eventually add up to a special privilege. Sometimes a deduction system is equally effective. Here the child starts with 'four

Most ADHD children are known for their call-outs and 'smart arse' comments.

lives', and if one remains at the end of class they leave with all their friends. If the lives have been spent they stay back for some minutes.

Touching and tapping

You can put a total ban on all clicking pens, but these children will still find something to tap, touch or jiggle. Fiddly fingers are so much part of the child's make-up, wise teachers accept the inevitable and teach them to jiggle quietly.

Changes – in-between times

A child with ADHD is not just overactive, they are over-active at the wrong times. They come in from the playground airborne, settle slowly, then wind up when they move again. It is this change from a calm, controlled environment to free play that causes the stress. There are no sure remedies but if we are prepared for these vulnerable times we can be on our guard.

- After a break the focus should be gradually increased with some general instruction, and when settled the child can move to the more complex work.

- There should be a warning five minutes before the end of class, allowing a gradual wind-down time.

■ School excursions can be an immense challenge due to the general level of hype and the loss of routine.

Overreacts to teasing

We often see gentle, sensitive children who are labelled 'aggressive'. They are not deliberately nasty, their problem is an overreaction to taunts and teasing. These children are sought out by school bullies, who stir them up.

Distraught parents often phone to say their child has been suspended. They tell of a predictable sequence of events. The ADHD child is happy and minding their own business, they are teased, they react, the bully enjoys the reaction and teases more, the ADHD child overreacts, the teacher makes a clumsy intervention, the blow-up escalates and the innocent child is suspended for three days.

Teachers need to be aware of this vulnerability of ADHD and soothe, not inflame. They need to look at the events at the start of play, rather than the final scene. We can suggest they count to 10 and turn the other cheek, but even intelligent adults find this difficult.

Teachers are there to help. They want to help. It's important for parents to show they are genuinely interested. Keep the lines of communication open. Don't always demand and criticise – *ask if you can help*.

THIRTEEN

Medication – The Facts

We make no apology for our enthusiasm for stimulant medication. The body of evidence is now so great that no reputable research centre questions the benefit and safety of this treatment in ADHD. We realise there are still anti-drug activists who claim medication is unhelpful and dangerous. As educated adults we recognise that the world is full of influential people who mislead through deliberate intent or through ignorance.

There may be people who dispute the facts about stimulant medication but the benefits are now so clearly documented, it is no longer worth debating the point.

Other therapies

The past 20 years have been an interesting time. First, we heard that ADHD would disappear when lead was removed from petrol, then we digressed into vitamin B6, multivitamins and, more recently, evening primrose oil, grapefruit juice, fish oil, omega-3 glyconutrients and various plant extracts.

One therapy has been around for the past 40 years: the relationship of diet to ADHD.

Diet and ADHD

If diet affects behaviour, it does so in children whether they do, or do not, have ADHD. It now seems that when diet works, its main effect is on activity and irritability. Those who work in the field of dietary management agree that diet is not the cause of ADHD but can make it worse.

Some parents do see changes with diet, but these are only with one or two clearly identified foods, such as chocolate, cola, some cordials, strawberries and some artificial colourings

Parents should never be prevented from following any remedy they choose. All we ask is that the well-researched, proven treatments are used first.

and flavourings. It must be emphasised that this is a minority, and the parents are usually quite clear about the offending food, so they avoid it. If there has been no obvious reaction to any one food, it is our experience that a strict exclusion diet will rarely bring any benefits.

The medications

It seems a piece of faulty logic to give a stimulant medication to a child who is already overstimulated, but this is just what they need. The stimulants, or more correctly the psychostimulants, are believed to work by

These medications are not sedatives – they do not dull a child's faculties.

increasing the neurotransmitter chemical dopamine in certain parts of the brain.

The stimulants methylphenidate (Ritalin) and dexamphetamine are the most commonly used and most effective preparations for the treatment of ADHD.

The use of stimulant medications for treating ADHD is not new. They were first shown to be effective in 1937, but were not widely used until the late 1950s

Stimulants allow the child to make use of their natural abilities to select, focus, shut out distraction and think before they act.

when methylphenidate (Ritalin) was first introduced. In the last half-century many parents have been frightened off stimulants by a media that branded them unsafe and controversial. The grounds for these anti-drug opinions never came from any scientific source. They originated with sensation-seeking journalists who were fed inaccurate information by pressure groups.

Ritalin and dexamphetamine – not quite the same

At present two stimulant preparations are used in Australia: methylphenidate (Ritalin) and dexamphetamine. It is said that these drugs are similar in effect, but in our clinical trials more than half the subjects will respond better to one medication than the other. Ideally both should be trialled, to ensure the child is getting the medication that best suits their individual needs.

Newer and longer acting methylphenidate preparations are also now available: Concerta and Ritalin LA.

Stimulants – absorption and action

The stimulants are in many ways similar to the Ventolin inhaler used in asthma. With Ventolin, you take a couple of puffs which kick in after 15 to 30 minutes, and in three to five hours the effect starts to wane. Similarly, stimulants start to work in about 30 minutes. The peak effect on behavioural learning starts to drop after three to five hours, with dexamphetamine usually lasting slightly longer and reach a fairly constant level in the blood. To exert their effect on the neurotransmitters they must cross the blood–brain barrier, a process that varies greatly from child to child.

Approximately half the original level of stimulant remains at the time that the next tablet is given. This is why we give most medication early in the morning and smaller doses as the day progresses. For example one tablet is given at breakfast, three-quarters of a tablet at midday and half a tablet at 3.30 pm. By 12 hours, almost all the stimulant has left the body. Stimulants are absorbed quickly even on a full stomach

The length of action or stimulant dosage is not influenced by other common medications such as antibiotics, paracetamol and anti-epileptics.

Are stimulants completely safe?

In medicine we must balance the benefits of treatment against the chance of any possible problem. The anti-stimulant activists forget that untreated ADHD is not without considerable risk.

As medicines go, the stimulants are exceptionally safe.

Every year, impulsive, unthinking children are seriously injured or even killed in preventable accidents. Parents and children fall out of love, this wrecked relationship continuing for life.

Clever children feel like failures, leaving school with a poor education, few friends and low esteem.

Proven short-term benefits

The action of stimulants has been studied extensively, most researchers reporting improvements in 70 to 90 per cent of children with ADHD. These are by far the most successful drugs used in child psychiatry and also the safest.

Work done by a 5-year-old off Ritalin

One week later: work done by same 5-year-old on Ritalin

Stimulants reduce restlessness, keep the child focused on a task, improve classroom productivity, and increase self-monitoring and accuracy. Children are less impulsive and disruptive, they learn when to back off. Written

Parents tell us they have a child who listens, takes instructions on board and can now accept reason.

work is neater and speech that once wandered may come back on track. Interactions improve between children, parents, teachers and peers.

Stimulants do not increase intelligence, though psychology tests may now be easier to administer. Specific learning disabilities, for example dyslexia, are not directly improved by stimulants, but once the dyslexic child starts to concentrate, the benefits of remediation increase. Stimulants do not treat the behaviours of ODD or CD, though curbing the impulsivity of ADHD may make these children safer and more predictable.

Long-term benefits

There is no doubt that the ADHD child treated with stim-

Stimulants do not increase the child's natural abilities, they just allow them to make the most of what they've got.

ulants is better today, tomorrow, next week, next month and next year. We know they are closer to their parents, happier in life, achieve at school and have more friends. It is our belief that if we get the short term right, this will follow through to the long term.

It has been shown conclusively that stimulants work in the short term; however, long-term gains are presumed but not proven. Most of the old studies did not distinguish between pure ADHD and ADHD with Conduct Disorder, this latter combination having a poor outcome, whether treated with medication or not. To resolve this we need objective, long-term studies, where some children with pure ADHD are treated and others left to fail, but nowadays this might be viewed as unethical.

When happier, less negative parents have a more responsive, rewarding child, this must provide a 'win–win' situation for all the players.

Eventually long-term results will show that with medication there is less nagging, negativity and anger.

Do ADHD children become addicted?

The word 'amphetamine' causes anxiety about addiction. Though stimulants have been used in ADHD children for some time, there is no evidence of addiction, dependency or an increased risk of later substance abuse. Treatment using the stimulants reduces later substance abuse by 80 to 85 per cent.

Stimulants – what parents notice

- Better able to sit and stick at task (computer, drawing, playing).
- Less impulsive (they think before they act or speak).
- Less insatiable (they can let a matter drop, do not go on and on).
- Listens, will back down, more accepting of frustration.
- Less restless, fidgety and 'full on'.
- More reachable, closer, happier.
- Interrupts less, and speech is more considered and on track.
- Home life becomes calmer.
- 'You have given us the child we always wanted.'

Stimulants – what teachers tell us

- Less distractable, disruptive and fidgety.
- Less calling out in class.
- Able to get work finished without the need to be stood over.
- Less rush, will check for mistakes.
- Produces neater written work which is more consistent and better organised.

- Shows improvement in playground behaviour.
- Relates better to other children, socially more in tune, has more friends.
- Grades improve. Confidence improves.

Children, adolescents and even adults with ADHD live their lives with a circling, muddled mind. When medication is effective they become clearer thinking and more focused. Humans take addictive drugs to escape the world, not to become fully focused on reality.

When to try stimulants

For years it has been policy to start with a behaviour program, and after some time to consider medication. This policy viewed stimulants as the back-stop, to be used when all else had failed. Current teaching does not agree – we now focus the child with medication and once we have a receptive subject, other treatments are introduced. Nowadays most children with major ADHD will start stimulants on their first visit.

A major US multi-centre study has recently completed research comparing the values of the different ADHD treatments. Six major university centres around the country compared the effects of very intensive behaviour/family

If you reach (with stimulants) then you are able to teach (with behaviour programs, therapy and schooling). and school-based therapy with medication that was either given alone or in combination with the intensive therapy. A fourth group was given 'community care', basically the use of medication without the close supervision and fine tuning of a specialist.

This milestone study spanning 14 months and involving 579 children found that treatments that don't prime first with medication are relatively unsuccessful. For more details, see *Understanding ADHD*.

What age can we treat?

Though most children treated with stimulants are of school age, there is no reason why medication cannot be used in the three to five year olds, as well as in the late teens and adults. We think carefully before prescribing in four year olds, but see great successes. The three to four year olds are only treated when the problems are causing great difficulty. Between two-and-a-half and three years a very small number of extreme children may be carefully considered for medication.

If the stimulants are tried and found ineffective in the under-fives they are worth reintroducing at an older age, as there may now be a positive response. In the mid-1980s high school children were taken off their medication in their early teens, which resulted in needless underachievement. Many children with ADHD will continue to take medication through their school years and into tertiary studies. And some will continue into adulthood.

FOURTEEN

Practical Prescribing

Before considering stimulants for the treatment of ADHD children, let's be quite clear that parents as well as the doctor decide if they want a trial of medication and when it should be continued or stopped. These drugs will be given while the parent sees major benefits and no side-effects. When there is doubt as to effectiveness, or the slightest concern over side-effects, parents must stop the drug and talk to the prescribing doctor.

The secret of successful prescribing is to start on a low dose and fine tune to the individual.

There is no black-and-white test that shows at what point stimulants should be prescribed. It all depends on the severity of the ADHD, the predominant behaviour, the degree of learning difficulties and how well both parents and school are managing. If education, home relationships, happiness and self-esteem are suffering, it's time to take a stand and start medication.

Start right – stay right

Introducing medication gradually and taking time to fine tune will always pay off. If you get it right at the start, it stays right.

If this also fails, we move to the second line of medications: non-stimulants, such as atomoxetine (Strattera).

Stimulants are remarkably free of side-effects. Any problems will come at the start of treatment or when doses are increased. Children rarely build up a tolerance to these drugs; if the dose is correct at the start, the same dose will often continue for some years.

Fine tuning stimulants

When methylphenidate and dexamphetamine are effective the benefits are almost immediate but last for only a very short time. There is an immense variation from child to child, some metabolising the drug very quickly and others showing response for much longer periods. For this reason fine tune stimulants to the individual.

It is extremely important for those monitoring the benefits of these treatments to be aware of this short span of action. If a tablet is given at 8 am and behaviour is disastrous in the early afternoon, this is not a failure of response – the child is not on active medication at the time of trouble. This is easily overcome by giving a second dose approximately half an hour before the time the first tablet starts to lose effect.

Fine tuning medication requires listening to parents and getting feedback from teachers.

Studies show that stimulants start to lose their effect when approximately half the level remains in the body. For this reason the second dose can be smaller than the first as it rides on top of the residual half that remains. Most children in our care have bigger doses at the beginning of the day, which tail off towards the afternoon.

Choosing the right number of doses depends on *what we are trying to treat*; for example, difficult behaviour that is present all day, concentrating on schoolwork from 9 am to 3 pm, behaviour at lunch break or problems with homework. Though some children do well on two doses per day, most are maintained on three: given at breakfast, the middle of the day and on returning from school. Some of our younger children require four to five smaller doses given two-and-a-half to three hours apart.

Just as the benefits of medication are almost immediate, most parents know the moment medication is starting to lose effect, which makes it easy to tune in a way which allows the best cover throughout the day.

The importance of this 'drop-off' cannot be overemphasised. We frequently see children in whom medication is said to have lost effect, when in fact it works wonderfully but there are behavioural blow-ups in the gaps between doses. This is not failure, it is a problem of fine tuning.

When stimulants don't work

Almost 90 per cent of those with a major degree of ADHD will respond to stimulant medication.

Though tolerance is extremely rare, occasionally a child stops responding for no apparent reason. When we suspect tolerance, we suspend the medication and observe what happens. Often the benefits are still there, but the parents had forgotten the way it used to be. If the dose has been re-tuned and the benefits have genuinely dropped off, then we trial another stimulant preparation.

One of the commonest causes of failure is a mis-understanding of what we are trying to treat. Stimulants help the deficiencies in attention and behaviour found in pure ADHD. Stimulants have no effect on the hostile attitudes of Oppositional Defiant Disorder or Conduct Disorder. Stimulants help the dyslexic child concentrate and work better, but they do not cure problems of reading. When there is no success with these comorbid conditions, this is a failure of expectation, not medication.

Do you need holidays off medicine?

If behaviour causes big problems, we never stop stimulants at home. In the early 1980s it was believed that long-term medication could retard a child's physical growth – this is no longer of concern. There is no evidence that properly monitored, long-term medication will in any way harm children. It is, however, certain that untreated ADHD children can do immense long-term damage to family relationships and to their own happiness.

Parents always ask us how long medication will be needed and the answer is simple: for as long as parents and teachers continue to see significant benefits. The parents we deal with are asked to continually monitor the benefits of stimulants. Most are aware of the drop-off after four hours and know when they forgot to give medication. If their child returns to the old ways this gives feedback as to the continuing need for stimulants. Remember the first words of this chapter: you, the parents, are in charge: *you, with the advice of the school, tell us whether medication will or will not be continued. It is your decision.*

FIFTEEN

Encouraging Self-esteem

ADHD is a real confidence crusher. If a child struggles at school, is socially inept and in trouble all the time, it is no wonder that esteem sinks. Of course, some ADHD children are so thick-skinned that they bounce through with remarkable resilience. Then there are those who star at sport, which helps shore up their confidence. Unfortunately, for most it is a hard road they tread, but one that can be made more comfortable if we boost, not crush, confidence.

Converting to confidence

For children to feel good about themselves, they must see that their words are valued, that their talents are appreciated and that they themselves are respected and trusted. At the same time, those who care for them need to encourage esteem, and in everything the focus must move from failure towards savouring success at something.

Wonderful words

Take time to listen as the ADHD child talks. Acknowledge what the child says, keep eye contact throughout the conversation and let them finish without interrupting. Show you're interested and let them know you care.

Well done

Take time to watch what they are doing, appreciate their effort and give help when it is needed. When things are not right, guide; *don't* criticise.

Be specific in your encouragement: 'The spelling is so much better'; 'This is the neatest paragraph'.

Respect and trust

Things may get spilt or broken and the work may be substandard, but at least the child is trying. Encourage them to do as much as they can without putting anyone at too much risk. Without responsibility and our trust, children feel inadequate and lack independence.

If you treat your children the way you would like to be treated yourself, you will never go far wrong.

Savouring success

A life which is all failure and no fun gets pretty depressing. As parents we need to look past the problems of school, to find hobbies, interests and outside

Confident children are those who savour success at something and it is up to us to find out what that something is.

activities our children enjoy. We must move the focus from what our children cannot do to what they *can* do.

Finding the right activity

At the end of the school day, the active ADHD child hits the outside world like an escaped prisoner. They want space, freedom, exercise and enjoyment. It is imperative that these school-stressed children have outside interests. It is up to parents to find what suits the child best.

Try: swimming, soccer and other team sports, bicycles, fishing, judo, tae kwan do, Scouts and other groups, athletics, cooking, acting, computer games.

Many ADHD children are uncomfortable in social situations. They look awkward, don't know what to say and feel out of place. As we plan outside interests, it is important to find ones that bring maximum enjoyment and minimal social stress.

The secret is to look for activities that give space and leave the child firmly in charge of their own communication. Those we have found most successful are bushwalking, bike riding and swimming.

Every ADHD child has some talent just waiting to be tapped. Parents need to be on the lookout for new activities and interests all the time. We must be patient, as ADHD children swing from immense enthusiasm to total turn-off in what seems like a millisecond. But don't give up, keep looking for new talents to encourage which will bring enjoyment and boost the child's esteem.

Parents must encourage these activities but not include too many lessons. It is wonderful when an ADHD child stars and has perfect style, but it is more important to enjoy than to excel.

SIXTEEN

Adults with ADHD

Adult ADHD first came to be noticed when paediatricians began to recognise that some of the parents of their patients had the same symptoms as their children. The idea of this adult condition took time to gain acceptance but it received the seal of approval when, in 1993, the main US parent support group changed its name to become Children and Adults with Attention Deficit Disorders.

The typical signs

- Inability to concentrate.

- Lack of organisation.

- Forgetfulness and poor memory.

- Poor self-discipline.

- Inability to establish and maintain a routine.

- Confusion, trouble thinking clearly.

- Inability to perform up to intellectual level in study.

- Performance on job below level of competence.

- Difficulty in finding and keeping jobs.

- Depression, low self-esteem.

It is believed that at least half of our ADHD children will bring some of the features of their condition into adulthood. Adult psychiatrists in North America, and to a lesser degree in Australia, New Zealand and the UK, now accept this as a real condition and are prepared to consider medication for its treatment.

Do we disclose?

It is rarely advisable to tell your workmates that you have a 'disorder'. There is, however, great advantage in being quite frank about your individual weak spots, for example: 'I have such a hopeless memory – I need to write things down'; 'Let's cool down – I'm a bit of a hot-head'; 'I'm pretty busy – I need to burn off some energy'; 'I've never been able to spell'. Approached in this way you are like everyone else, just with a greater scattering of strengths and weaknesses.

Despite the current interest in ADHD, we see many parents who are unaware that this condition was the cause of their troubles in childhood. One of the saddest parts of our work is to meet intelligent, talented adults who still believe they are inferior, inadequate and dumb. It is criminal that this unnecessary assault on their esteem was ever allowed to take place. We can't change the past, but we can be doubly determined that the same will never happen to the ADHD children of this present generation.

Help for Parents

Australian Support Groups

There are now many support groups all over Australia. Following is a list of the main organisations in each state. They will provide you with the name of the closest group in your area.

ACT
Canberra/Queanbeyan Support Group
PO Box 717
Mawson ACT 2607
Ph: (02) 6290 1984
Fax: (02) 6286 4475
Email: infor@addact.org.au
Website: www.addact.org.au

NSW
LD Coalition of NSW Inc.
PO Box 140
Westmead NSW 2145
Ph: (02) 9806 9960
Fax: (02) 9806 9940
Email: ldcoalitionnsw@ozemail.com.au
Website: www.learning difficultiescoalition.org.au

Adults with ADHD of NSW Inc.
PO Box 140
Westmead NSW 2145
Ph: (02) 9806 9960
Fax: (02) 9806 9940

Email: rossleonard@netspace.net.au

QLD
ADDAQ
PO Box 1661
Milton QLD 4064
Ph: (07) 3368 3977
Fax: (07) 3849 7987
Email: addiss@bigpond.com.au
Website: www.users.bigpond.com/addiss

SA
ADASA
195 Gilles Street
Adelaide SA 5000
Ph: (08) 8232 0685
Fax: (08) 8232 0687
Email: karyl_ranse@hotmail.com

TAS
C Diedrichs
PO Box 7627
Launceston TAS 7250
Email: cdiedric@bigpond.net.au

VIC
Active Inc.
Ross House
247 Flinters Lane
Melbourne Vic 3000
Ph: (03) 9650 2570
Email: active@vicnet.net.au
Website: www.avoca.vicnet.
net.au/~active

WA
LADS
The Niche - Suite B
11 Aberdare Road
Nedlands WA 7544
Ph: (08) 9346 7544
Fax: (08) 9346 7545
Email: lads@cnswa.com
Website: www.ladswa.com.au

NZ Support Groups

ADDvocate NZ Inc.
PO Box 249
Tauranga
National Co-ordinator:
Charles Harrison
Ph: (07) 577 0987
Fax: (07) 571 0901
Email: addvocate@xtra.co.nz
Website: www.adhd.org.nz
The above website has contact
details of groups in most areas
throughout New Zealand.

ADHD Association
PO Box 51–675
Pakuranga
Auckland

Ph: (09) 570 5646
Email: adhd@xtra.co.nz
This group has contacts in most
areas of New Zealand.

Teenadders Inc.
PO Box 54
Red Beach
Whangaparoa
Ph: (09) 426 0595
Email: teenadders@xtra.co.nz
Website: www.teenadders.org.nz
Specialists in dealing with
teenagers with ADHD

Note: The authors believe the support group contacts to be correct as of March 2004. As these are run by volunteers, details will change over time but aim to revise regularly. We urge you to respect the time and privacy of those listed.

Index